Nina Chiba. –

WCC

MW01678496

Listen to the Women!

Listen to the Earth!

opp. Christmas Hotel – 11am.
(School) [illegible] – phone – 5833853

St George's. + Maurine.
U.S. group.
Jeff Halper –
Arik Asherman.
Anglican Church of Canada partnership ē the Ang. Cathedral – Jerusalem.

Listen to the Women!

Listen to the Earth!

Aruna Gnanadason

Risk BOOK

WCC Publications, Geneva

The cover image of a woman embracing a tree symbolizes the Chipko movement, a largely women-led movement in the Himalayan region of India where the villagers clung to the trees to protest commercial felling. The doll was designed and made by Sr Françoise Bosteels of Belgium, of the Order of the Sisters of the Divine Saviour, who has worked in India for over thiry years. We acknowledge with thanks her permission to use this image.

Cover design: Marie Arnaud Snakkers
Cover photo: Peter Williams

ISBN 2-8254-1472-7

150 route de Ferney, P.O.Box 2100
1211 Geneva 2
Switzerland
Website: http://www.wcc-coe.org

No. 111 in the Risk Book Series

Printed in Switzerland

Table of Contents

To Jonathan, my husband,
for his encouragement and support at all times

and
to the women of Deomali Women's Society,
Koraput, Orissa, for their courage

Words of Thanks

This book is a reworking of my thesis for the doctorate of ministries from San Francisco Theological Seminary. The text has been shortened, transformed into this form, updated and re-edited. I would like to place on record my thanks to Letty Russell and Shannon Clarkson who lead the international feminist theologies DMin programme for having been an important source of encouragement and support. I also express gratitude to William Stanley and Sasi Prabha Stanley for organizing my several visits to Koraput, Orissa, and for sharing with me a glimpse of their commitment and passion for the work they do among the Indigenous peoples in that part of India. To all the Indigenous women of the Deomali Women's Society, Koraput, Orissa, who spoke to me, I extend appreciation and thanks for the time they gave me and for their courage in their struggles.

My thanks too to Konrad Raiser, the immediate past general secretary of the World Council of Churches, for his support, and to Samuel Kobia, the present general secretary, who ensured all the time and resources I needed to complete this work. To a host of friends in India and in Geneva who supported me through this, my special thanks. To each member of the Justice, Peace and Creation team of the WCC my deep gratitude not just for their understanding when I was away writing but for all the love and care they have offered whenever I was down or anxious. Their humour at times when it was needed, but also their passion and commitment for the work we do, is what kept me inspired. A special word of thanks to Laura Sandoval Merritt for her special computer skills with which she helped me format the text and make the manuscript look presentable. To Martin Robra, my colleague and friend, my special thanks for all the time he spent with me reading and rereading what I wrote and advising me on ways to strengthen the text or to organize my thoughts. His knowledge of materials and particularly of WCC documents has been invaluable. I enjoyed the long conversations with him. His critical and creative mind helped me clarify my own thoughts.

Finally, I express my deep appreciation to all our family in India, to Jonathan my husband and to our sons Chittaranjan and Uday, and to Runa, my daughter-in-law, for their patience and endurance. Without your urging me on, I may not have completed this work. I therefore dedicate this book to Jonathan and to all of them, with affection and deep thanks.

Geneva
29 April 2005

1. Prudent Care and an Ethic of Resistance

For us, the rivers, the forests and our land
are the basis of our existence.
This earth is our mother.
No one can snatch her away from us.
No one has the right
to take away our land from us.

We therefore take an oath today
that we will always protect
our land and rivers.
Large dams being built in this area
are drowning our forests,
our mountains and our land.

We pledge never to let this happen.[1]

Every year, when we visit the ancestral village of our family, we see more changes and more of the "take-over" of Mother Earth by those who have the power and the money to do so. Thittuvillai is a small village in the southern-most part of India. Some ten years ago it was still "a little piece of heaven on earth". Rich greenery – paddy fields and the verdant mountain range of the Western Ghats – surround this little village. It is a region that has thrived for centuries steeped in mythology and nature-affirming folk tales. *Thadagathi* is one of these mountains... she is in fact a slain "demon queen" (according to a popular version of the story), killed by the Lord Rama, one of the leading figures in the epic Ramayana.

Thadagathi was the reigning queen of the region. She was dark-skinned and "ugly" according to the standards of the invading Aryan culture, and became a "demon" in their eyes. She undoubtedly represents the Dalit peoples[2] of India. The story goes that Rama was hunting in the region, on his way to Lanka to save his abducted queen Sita from the hands of her abductor the king of Lanka, Ravana. *Thadagathi* challenged Rama and asked him to desist from killing the wildlife of the territory she ruled over. Rama was not used to having his authority challenged by anyone, let alone by a dark-skinned "ugly" woman, and so he killed her. He is said to have deeply regretted having killed a woman, but he had his way. Read from the perspective of Dalit history the story can be given a whole new interpretation based on principles of respect and a protective attitude to the earth and the things of the earth.

Thadagathi lies there as a mountain, serene and majestic, having lost out to the selfish greed of the powerful one who considered hunting to be his birthright. *Thadagathi* lies there dead, reminding India of all that we are losing! The Western Ghats are, year after year, losing their greenery – the mountains are being mined for granite and other minerals and are threatened altogether to disappear. A region which has for centuries survived with its mountain streams and lakes, blessed in the protective care of *Thadagathi*, is now slowly dying. The water is being channelled into the neighbouring district, to water the Koodankulam nuclear reactor and other industrial projects. The paddy fields are slowly disappearing as the struggling farming community is forced to sell out and the nearby town spreads rapidly into the countryside, one more symbol of the dying India. But *Thadagathi* lies there still, reminding us daily of the power of the people who live with the earth. This mythological story is reflective of the traditions of prudent care that persist in all parts of the country.

Myth, tradition and care for creation

Such prudent practices can be found in several areas of India where Indigenous peoples live. Indigenous peoples in India are called *Adivasis*, a word which, literally translated, means "the first inhabitants or peoples of the land". Among them is found the concept of *sarna* that refers to the few kilometres of forest land, maintained by the community as protected land. It is believed that the spirits of the ancestors reside here. Initiation rites of teenagers of Indigenous communities are normally held here. In other parts of the country sacred groves are known as *devaranya* (God's abode) or *nagaranya* (the abode of cobras). Here *peepal* and *mahua* trees (indigenous varieties) cannot be cut as they are considered to be the abodes of goddesses. The tiger is considered a totem and hence should not be killed.

Two Indian environmental scientists, Madhav Gadgil and Ramachandra Guha, propose that the prudent care of the earth should reflect genuine efforts at restraint by following communitarian rules and regulations. There is a quantitative restriction on the amount harvested of a given species, or of that which is harvested from a given locality. Certain habitat patches may be abandoned. Harvesting of some species or from a specific habitat may be abandoned. Some stages of life – categorized by age, sex, size or reproductive status – may immunize an animal or bird from being harvested. Selected species may never be harvested either because of the relative difficulty of procuring them (risk or injury during the hunt) or because they carry parasites that can affect humans. Specified habitat patches may never be harvested or be subject to very low levels of harvest through strict regulations. Providing refuge through sacred groves, sacred ponds, etc. may be the most easily perceived and most efficient way of guarding against resource depletion.

This system of environmental ethics provides for communities a code of moral guidelines for environmental protection and conservation – to be followed by common people and also by kings and rulers. A great deal of locality-specific knowledge of bio-diversity resides with "eco-system peoples" and is significant to their life-styles. "Eco-system peoples" refers to Indigenous peoples, Dalits, etc. who live in a protective relationship with the land. This, for instance, is the case with specialist fisher-folk, who have an intimate knowledge of water bodies and ongoing changes in them with their snail, bivalve, shrimp, crab and other fish and fauna inhabitants. Nomadic shepherds know a great deal about large tracts of scrub savannahs and grasslands and their vegetation. This knowledge can and should be tapped to feed into a wider process of diversity conservation.[3]

There is a deep spirituality associated with the traditions of prudent care – most of these traditions can be dated to pre-Aryan days in India and to mother goddesses.[4] Scientists assess that there are some 100,000 sacred groves in India that are being protected by communities and village government systems. A large majority of sacred groves are associated with female village deities. But with the gradual take-over of the groves by Hindu groups, women as priests ministering to the groves are rare, and women are in many cases not even permitted to enter the groves after reaching an age of menstruation as they are then considered polluting.[5]

"Traditions of prudence" depend on two conditions. First, that some other lineage does not usurp the resource when it becomes available; and second, that the resource should continue to be of value to the lineage adopting prudence. There are cases cited by ecologists in India to substantiate this. The Dheevar caste of the Bhandara district of Maharashtra never catch fish going upstream on spawning migration, although the fish are exhausted and easy to catch. There are entire sacred groves and ponds in which no plant or animal is damaged – some species of plants and animals survive only in such protected localities. Monkeys, peafowl, the banyan and fig trees and a variety of plants and animals are regarded as sacred and are protected widely in many parts of India. In the village of Kokre-Bellur in the southern state of Karnataka, birds that are breeding are left undisturbed.

Hinduism offers the concept of *vasudhaiv kutumbakam* (the family of Mother Earth) that is closely interconnected with the understanding of *sarva-bhuta-hite-ratah* (to serve all beings equally). This is described as "*dharmic* ecology" with its origins in the Hindu Vedic heritage. This environmental model draws from the Hindu concept of *dharma* (a set of duties that hold the social and moral fabric of a society together) and *karma* (actions and the effects of such actions) and provides new ways of valuing and acting with the earth. It is believed that "*dharma* if universally manifested will provide the values necessary for an environmentally caring world and will not advance economic growth at the cost of greed, poverty, inequality and environmental degradation.

There is an urgent need to instil in all people a respect for nature and to strengthen the decision-making processes in favour of environmental protection. The Hindu religion, like many other religions and spiritual traditions, has the capacity to move the individual towards the divine because of its belief in divinity in nature."[6]

Reverence for trees pervades Hindu literature. Laws for the protection of plants and trees can be found in ancient sacred Hindu texts. Plants are seen as sentient beings that have consciousness and therefore should be protected from harm. The designation of certain trees as sacred objects because of their religious value, identified with certain deities, protects these tree varieties. Ironically, the respect for some trees includes the economic value of that particular tree. A certain penance was prescribed for the cutting down of trees – in proportion to the value of the tree.[7] Vandana Shiva speaks of how the forests have been worshipped as *Aranyani* (the goddess of the forest):

> The sacred tree serves as an image of the cosmos, a symbol of the inexhaustible source of cosmic fertility. The earth mother as primordial Mother says: "O ye gods, I shall support (i.e. nourish) the whole world with life sustaining vegetables which shall grow out of my body, during the period of heavy rain. I shall gain fame on earth then as Shakhambari (goddess who feeds the herbs), and in that very period, I shall slay the great *asura* named Durgama (a personification of drought)" (Devimahatmya 90:43-44).[8]

Feminine energy

In pre-Aryan thought, nature was symbolized as the embodiment of the feminine *shakthi* (energy, power). *Prakriti* (nature) manifests this primordial energy from which women draw their *shakthi*. Concepts such as *Bhudevi* (Earth Goddess) and *Bhumata* (Mother Earth) that are used in people's everyday language underline this. Vandana Shiva quotes the words of Itwari Devi, a woman leader in the struggle against mining operations in the Utharkhand region of the Himalayan mountains:

> Our power is nature's power; our *shakthi* (power) comes from *prakriti* (nature). Our power against the contractor comes from

> these inner sources, and is strengthened by his trying to oppress and bully us with his false power of money and muscle. We have offered ourselves, even at the cost of our lives, for a peaceful protest to close this mine, to challenge and oppose the power that the government represents. Each attempt to violate us had strengthened our integrity. They stoned our children and hit them with iron rods, but they could not destroy our *shakthi*.[9]

Similar concepts can be found in Buddhism too. Buddhist iconography gives form to the multiple sentient beings of the trees, the air, the waters, and the earth. Islam speaks of the earth as a Mother who needs periodic rest.[10]

Taking a more critical approach to Hindu attitudes to the earth, environmentalist Anil Agarwal recognizes anthropomorphism in Hinduism too. He describes the relationship of Hindus to the earth as a form of "utilitarian conservationism" and not as "protectionist conservationism". This implies that Hindus value and protect those features of nature that "have gained significance within the ritual cycle of human flourishing".[11] He critiques Hinduism for being a highly individualistic religion. According to him, *dharma*, as a system of social responsibility, focuses on one's own behaviour, for the sake of one's own well-being first – one's behaviour to others plays a secondary role. Therefore personal hygiene takes prior position in a Hindu home; the garbage outside the door is ignored. "The streets around Hindu upper-caste settlements are often dirtier than poor tribal villages."[12] However, Agarwal believes that Hinduism too can become an earth faith. In his understanding the hope for Hinduism lies in its reform in response to the present context. He has this hope because within the "eclectic nature of Hinduism, there is a vast reservoir of tenets, practices and beliefs that can help Hindus to reform Indian society".[13]

Women as voices of prudence

Women have played a central role in the traditions of prudence in India, but women as bearers of prudence is not a phenomenon specific to India alone. Rosemary Radford Ruether writes of women as the mediators and caretakers of nature, drawing on the experiences of poor women of Latin America or the Dalits and women of the fishing communities in India; the Indigenous peoples of the Himalayan regions of India, the Cordillera in the Philippines or from Guatemala, or the women in Kenya, Zimbabwe or Southern Africa – all offer experiences of women healing earth. Gladys Parentelli from Venezuela says, "The practices described are not simply quaint, isolated habits."[14] They are the life-struggles of women who have been at the centre of traditional practices of care of creation and women engaging in protests to protect the earth. Their experiences are situated in a wealth of myths, stories and religious practices from various Indigenous faith traditions and some from interpretations and reappropriations of an inherited Christianity.

It is important to reflect on why a discussion on the death of nature, and the urgency to listen to voices of prudence, have become urgent today. This book will trace some of the traditions of prudence as well as resistance against the onslaughts on the earth, and share what inspires women's activism; but in addition it will show how the context in India is linked globally, taking the issue of water as an example, and will identify what the ecumenical movement can learn from this. The book also underlines that religions, especially Christianity, need to become more earth-caring.

First, a brief overview of India's ecological context: According to government of India statistics, 19.7 percent of the country's geo-area is *forested* (as opposed to the desired target of 33 percent as stipulated in the 1988 national forest policy) and is presently declining at an estimated 1.3 million hectares a year. The average annual availability of *water* per capita has declined from 5236 cubic metres in 1951 to 2464 cubic metres at present. It is estimated that by 2017, India will be a water-stressed country, because the per capita water availability will be as low as 1600 cubic metres. Ground water exploitation is increasing rapidly (both for qualitative and quantitative reasons), resulting in the decline of the water table in most places. The number of tube wells has increased from 0.3 million in 1967 to 6 million in 1997. Again, according to official estimates, in 1980, 56.6 percent of the land suffered from environmental degradation, especially water and wind erosion. In some canal projects, one half of the area that could have been irrigated and cultivated has been lost due to water-logging. The area under periodic floods doubled between 1971 and 1981. The soil is losing its fertility due to excessive use of chemical fertilizers. Fertilizer and pesticide run-offs into natural water sources have destroyed fish life and have polluted water for human use in several areas. Water pollution is India's worst environmental problem – it is estimated that 70 percent of India's surface water resources are severely polluted – including urban discharges into water and toxic and other pollutants, especially heavy metals by industries.

Urban *air pollution* is increasing due to power consumption, industrialization, vehicle-use and refuse-burning (automobile production reached 4.6 million units in 1997-1998). India is the world's sixth largest (and second fastest-growing) source of greenhouse gas emissions. The per capita carbon dioxide emissions in 1996 were estimated at 1.1 metric tons. Fuel combustion accounts for 66 percent of the total carbon dioxide emissions, followed by change in land use and forestry, cement manufacture and vehicular emissions. The annual generation of non-hazardous waste by industry is 90 million tons, and of hazardous waste 9.3 million tons. Finally the rapid increase in India's urbanization has placed tremendous pressure on water supply, waste-water treatment, air quality and solid-waste management.[15]

India as a country has been hailed for being among the fastest growing economies in the world – at what cost, one must ask. Gadgil and Guha make a historical overview of what has made India into what they term "a fissured land".[16] Perhaps for the first time, they retell the history of ancient, medieval and modern India from the perspective of ecology. Traditional historians often ignore this perspective on the history of a nation. Gadgil and Guha underline that the ecological fabric of a society influences human relationships as well as the politics of land- and resource-use and is therefore of critical importance in understanding the history of a nation. They write both of traditions of prudent care of the earth and its resources in this history, but also of the more predominant profligacy with which the resources have been exploited.

In the industrial period of development, over the last two hundred years, the ecological impact has been profound. In one-fiftieth of the time since animal domestication and plant cultivation was started and one one-hundredth of the time since the hunter-gathering mode of development emerged, resource-use and depletion has been rapid. There has been a quantum leap in the use of non-renewable resources (coal and oil) as well as entirely new sources of energy such as nuclear energy. While strides in transportation, resources and production flows have become global, the inequalities in the world have also become starker. Locally adapted life-styles in different parts of the world have virtually been wiped out. The hypothetical deductive method of modern Western science has been linked with practical applications in order to tap more sources of energy to process materials and transport goods faster. This has led to the continuous over-use and exhaustion of many resources. With the exhaustion of their own resources, European colonialists laid claim to vast terrains the world over, and set in place the asymmetrical flows of goods, people and resources. But at every stage the people most affected by resource depletion have resisted the developments – and women have played a key role here.

Women-centred movements of political struggles

Women-centred movements of political struggles to protect the earth are rooted in these traditions of prudence. Throughout Indian history there have been movements of resistance by communities in a bid to protect the earth. One of the best-known movements took place in 1451 (over 500 years ago), in the midst of the Bishnoi group of people, in the Thar Desert of Rajasthan in North West India. This community gave absolute protection to the *khejadi (proposis cinerarea)*, a multipurpose leguminous, traditional tree, as it is of great importance to the villagers. The Bishnois were never known to uproot or kill a *khejadi* tree, nor would they allow anyone from outside to uproot or kill the trees in their villages. The account goes that the prince of Jodhpur needed wood to fuel his lime-kilns and to provide for the energy needs of the palace. He also needed the fuel to build a new palace and therefore ordered that a grove of *khejadi* trees be felled. It is said that the women of the village clung to the trees, defying the saws of the royal soldiers. Many women were killed and the soldiers finally had to stop the felling operations because other villagers immediately took the place of the fallen ones to protect their trees. The tree was sacred to the people, yet it was of value to them too. Its pods, leaves and thorny branches provided food, fodder, manure and fencing materials.

This was the movement that inspired two recent environmental movements – Chipko and Apiko – both of which follow a similar form of resistance to the cutting of trees for commercial purposes. Here too, women clung to the trees in order to protect them from the companies attempting to fell them. These largely Indigenous women-led movements have contributed not just to protecting a particular region of the country but have also played an influential role in environmental movements in other parts of the country.

Two women-led protest movement

The Deomali Mahila Society of Indigenous women in Koraput, Orissa, and the Narmada Bachao Andolan (Save the Narmada Movement) to protect the river Narmada from the mega-dam projects are two such protest movements in which women have played a pivotal role. The Deomali Adivasi Mahila Society (Deomali Indigenous Women's Society) is led by Indigenous and Dalit women in the Koraput region of Orissa, and grew out of their strong determination to challenge the many injustices they experience. The women have organized themselves against the pressures of "development", social forestry which promotes "foreign" tree varieties and mining operations, but also against the extra burdens they face in their families and community because they are women.

As traditional structures of Indigenous and Dalit community life break down, women lose some of the traditional rights they have enjoyed in their communities. Women do most of the back-breaking work and are paid less than men. Women most often sacrifice everything for the sake of their families. Health care offered by the government is virtually non-existent. Women's roles in decision-making in the family and community is minimal. And to add to this, they experience violence at the hands of many men in their families.

Sonia Pongi and the other women of her community in Semiliguda in the Koraput district of Orissa watched the way in which their lives were falling apart around them, and how some of their own kith and kin exploited each other. They saw the way in which the "civilizing" influence of those who came from outside threatened to destroy them. The outsiders came with their English schools, cinema houses and "urban ways". They recognized that as women they were experiencing specific forms of discrimination and violence.

The women organized themselves and came together to talk about what was happening around them and decided to take control of their lives. They formed themselves into the Deomali Adivasi Mahila Society (significantly they took the name of the beloved and sacred mountain in their region, Deomali, to give them their identity as a federation of Indigenous and Dalit women). Each village has its own group and deals with the issues or struggles most relevant to it. They meet together regularly as a federation to share each other's struggles and strategies. The women were not able to get rid of the national aluminium factory and other industrialization projects, nor were they able to stop the mining operations in their area – for that they were too late – but their actions against these developments brought the community together. Men and women of the Indigenous and Dalit communities living there decided that they had to try to reclaim some of their values and to rebuild their lives. They are on their way to re-educating their children to respect the traditional ways of life and to live in harmony with each other and with creation. Production of their traditional handicrafts and marketing their goods is a way in which they reclaim their traditions. Efforts are being made to restore their traditional wisdom regarding the medicinal value of certain herbs and plants. Additionally, the women are now fighting for equal wages with the men and against the production and sale of country-made liquor in their villages. They have also managed to acquire rights to own property in their own names or jointly with their husbands. The women have been elected into *Panchayats* (local government) bodies.

Sonia Pongi and her sisters know what environmental degradation is. In the social forestry programmes offered by the government only traditional tree varieties that are environmentally friendly are planted. The women are fully involved with their men in deciding alternatives in the field of agriculture, irrigation systems, medicines and technology as well as disaster management. The government, in collusion with industrialists, bureaucrats and upper-caste and upper-class peoples, could suffocate them and take away from them all they believe in. The women work closely with the organization of Indigenous peoples who have been resisting the industrialization of the region.

According to Amnesty International, the organization of Indigenous peoples in this district has been perceived by the Indian government as being involved in "criminal activities and had incited tribal people to violence to prevent the establishment of industrial projects in the district".[17] Amnesty International has recognized that the Koraput district of Orissa is populated by a large percentage of Indigenous peoples who have been marginalized in the last fifty years, during which thousands of hectares of land have been taken over from the local populations for industries and mines. Several multinational companies are now involved in investing in this region rich in bauxite, to extract the ore and process it. Amnesty International protests against the use of force by the government to stop the legitimate demonstrations of the Indigenous peoples against these onslaughts on their lives and emphasizes their right to economic, social and cultural rights. Amnesty has considered this struggle as important enough to call for intervention to support it. But the use of force is indicative of the power of the powerful to take over and "develop" the Indigenous lands at all costs – even at the denial of the civil rights of Indigenous populations.[18] For those living on the edge of survival, as for the millions of the Indigenous and Dalit communities in India, protection of nature is protection of life itself.

The Save the Narmada River movement

The Narmada Bachao Andolan (Save the Narmada River movement) is a struggle against the damming of the river Narmada, one of the longest rivers in India that flows for 1300 kms through three states of India – Madhya Pradesh, Maharashtra and Gujarat – and empties itself into the Arabian Sea. The multi-million dam project includes plans to build 3200 dams on this river and its 41 tributaries. Thirty will be major dams, 135 medium-sized dams and the rest small. This project is altering the ecology of this river valley: it is leading to the massive displacement and disruption of life and livelihood of some 25 million Indigenous peoples and will submerge 4000 square kms of deciduous forestlands.

The protests began in the early 1980s led by several people including a woman activist, Medha Patkar. The dam project eroded traditional ways of the people – particularly of women. Informal trade links, local barter systems, labour markets and the complex social relationships providing avenues for representation, mediation and conflict resolution have all been disrupted. Additionally, ancestral sacred zones or graves and temples have been desecrated, the scattering of the people has disrupted and kinship groups, family systems and informal social networks that provide mutual support have become disorganized. This forced displacement has resulted in a spiral of impoverishment. Activists point out that for women, networks connected with place are crucial because they provide social support, financial assistance and shelter in times of distress. These systems cannot be easily replicated in resettlement sites.

One of their demands is to be compensated for the land they have lost. This is complicated because Indigenous communities do not have the papers to prove that they owned the land in the first place. Traditionally they did not "own" land as the land belonged to the whole community. And in attempts to address ownership, women have been left on the sidelines. When the government decides to regularize land ownership and registers the land with legal documents, the head of the family is given the papers to indicate their legal rights over the land, ignoring the fact that the investment of property rights to the men does not automatically imply that Indigenous women will be compensated. The issue of intra-family inequalities is not often taken seriously when land is redistributed. Considering that in rural India it is estimated that a third of women between the ages of eighteen and thirty are deserted or leave their husbands, female-headed households are still not recognized when land is redistributed. To Bina Agarwal, "The gender gap in the ownership and control of property is the single most critical contributor to the gender gap in economic well-being, social status and empowerment. In primarily rural economies such as those of South Asia the most important property in question is arable land."[19] Women have often been in the forefront of demonstrations, because of their ability to endure personal hardship (Mohandas Gandhi used the same logic in involving women in the freedom movement).

As in many other places in the world, governmental projects refuse to recognize that Indigenous peoples have their own ways of life and that they cannot be streamlined into the life-styles of the dominant groups because they are so different from them culturally and socially.

> In fact displaced tribals are thrust into an alien context which "others" them and seeks to absorb them completely into the lowest levels of society and economy... Tribal women, especially, bear the brunt of sexual attacks and harassment. These are justified by the attackers who see tribal women as "loose".

> Since women's wages are crucial for displaced populations, tribal women most likely face sexual advances in their everyday work. In fact, the lack of employment opportunities combined with social stigma has led many tribal women to prostitution.[20]

The movement has been inspired by an Indigenous cosmology that respects the earth as mother, as life-giving and life-sustaining and resists the desacralization of sacred sites. "Our links with our ancestors are the basis of our society and of the reproduction of our society. Our children grow up playing around the stones which mark the burial sites of our ancestors."[21]

Arundathi Roy, the Booker Prize-winning author and writer, draws attention to the plight of those displaced by dams who now earn a few rupees a day (less than a dollar) to stay alive. They have been alienated from the forest on which they depended and which had traditionally provided all they needed – food, fodder, fuel, rope, gum, tobacco, medicinal herbs, housing materials and even tooth powder – they now have lost it all.

> Instead of a river, they have a hand pump. In their old villages, they had no money, but they were insured. If the rains failed, they had the forest to turn to. The river to fish in. Their livestock was their fixed deposit. Without all this they are a heartbeat away from destitution.[22]

All this is indeed violence against the people who will be displaced. It is intentional death to the land. It is an intentional way to break a people's sacred bond with the earth. "To slow a beast, you break its limbs. To slow a nation, you break its people. You rob them of volition. You demonstrate your absolute command over their destiny. You make it clear that it ultimately falls to you to decide who lives, who dies, who prospers, who doesn't. To exhibit your capability you show off all you can do, and how easily you can do it. How easily you could press a button and annihilate the earth. How you can start a war, or sue for peace. How you can snatch a river away from one and gift it to another. How you can green a desert or fell a forest and plant one somewhere else. You use caprice to fracture a people's faith in ancient things – earth, forest, water, air."[23]

The big dams have eroded traditional systems of maintaining water resources and careful use of smaller village tanks and tributaries. All over India, village tanks have been taken over by the government-run minor irrigation department, leading to the collapse of local management systems and the "dying" of the ponds due to silting. Impact studies of different dam projects have shown that the ecological and social costs far surpassed the benefits, and "typically, the benefits were grossly exaggerated in order to accommodate the World Bank's logic of returns of investment".[24]

The struggle to save the Narmada continues... more Indigenous protestors are killed; more efforts are made to displace the people forcibly. And yet, the spirit of resistance of the people will not be suppressed!

Caught between layers of the economy

Women's actions for justice and for the protection of the earth give just a small glimpse of what women in India and all over the world are engaged in. The many ways in which power is abused could lead to a feeling of despair and hopelessness, but to the women in resistance struggles there is no other alternative but to refuse to give in. The Indigenous woman's energy comes from her understanding of the earth as mother who will protect her and her people and will nurture them. Therefore to reappropriate motherhood as an ethical value is a way forward. But this requires critiquing the way patriarchy has used it and distorted its interpretation.

Narango Puri, an Indigenous woman leader from the Deomali Adivasi Mahila Association, speaks of what gives women like her the inspiration and courage to continue in the struggle despite the forces that attempt to destroy them. To Narango,

> Life starts on the land for the woman, from the moment she is born. She wakes up each day on the land and the rivers, trees, birds are also living on the land – they are all our relatives... There is a relationship between the woman and the land – that

> is why we begin cultivating the land only after we worship the mother, i.e. the land... Earth is like our mother. As humans we go through the life-cycle – we give birth, we nurture our young ones at the breast, we grow and we die. The earth will never die, but this requires that we as women who also go through the same processes of birthing and caring for our children need to also nurture the earth.[25]

What message of hope can we gain from the wisdom of Narango and the millions of women like her?

Women and the poor are the ones caught between layers of the economy. In spite of their deep respect and love for the earth, it has to be acknowledged that, while it is the poor Indigenous and Dalit women who are the worst affected by this loss of basic resources, they are often the agents of resource depletion because of forces they can scarcely understand, still less control.[26] When pushed to the limit a poor person will opt for shelter for the family as a priority. A poet poignantly describes this reality:

> *Right*
> I will not stop cutting down trees
> Though there is life in them
> I will not stop plucking out leaves,
> Though they will make nature beautiful
> I will not stop hacking off branches,
> Though they are the arms of a tree
> Because –
> I need a hut.[27]

An example of resource depletion by the poor is of a village of Gopeshwar in the Garhwal region of the Himalayas. Here each part of the community would normally carefully observe traditional regulations regarding the quantity of plant bio-mass that is allowed to each family from a grove of oak and other broad-leaved species of trees. But since the allowed quantity is not enough for their needs, for the remainder they turn to other hill slopes where exploitation is unregulated and denudation is at an advanced stage. This was not the case some decades ago, when the grove was larger and fulfilled the demands of a smaller population in a sustainable way – now they have to go elsewhere and take what they need with no controls.[28]

Some Indigenous communities that have strict customary laws regarding the cutting of trees are now forced to engage in ecocide due to abject poverty and alienation from the forests they love, which have for centuries been the source of their life and livelihood. Poverty leads to this. This tension between various layers of the economy leaves no choice to the poor – whether they want to or not, they are forced into the dominant monetarized economy and have to participate in its exploitative allurements.

An example of a life-giving alternative as the people take control

But this does not undermine the role that Indigenous communities are playing in caring for the resources of the earth. Sometimes this comes through the search for alternatives to the exploitative ways of big industries and so called development projects. The efforts of the Indigenous community in Putsil, organized by the Weaker Sections Integrated Development Project, India, under the leadership of William Stanley and Sasi Prabha, is an example. Putsil is a small village situated in the heart of the mountain range called the Eastern Ghats in Orissa, India. The village of Putsil with a population of 370 is located at an altitude of 1150 metres above sea level. Like all other villages in the region, Putsil has been in perpetual darkness and the people have had to depend on oil lamps and kerosene lanterns. However, the Indigenous peoples who live here have been organized to convert an already existing small dam into a mini hydroelectric project. The community has been fully involved in the setting up of this project, and not a single tree was cut in the process.

Each house has been supplied with 60 kilowatts (kW) of electricity – a power line for one or two bulbs. Some have even managed to set up TV sets in their homes. This small plant produces just enough electricity for Putsil – just 5640 kW during the night and 3000 kW in daytime. The villagers decided to share the power with a neighbouring village, providing a battery-charging facility for them. A perennial stream provides water for the production of power and it is ensured that water for the generation of power is taken after the needs for agricultural production are met. The villagers gave their labour as their contribution and now two young people have been trained to run the power plant. It is completely managed by the people. The women have been in the forefront of this movement: the second major use of the electricity is to run a grinding and milling machine. Women who had spent back-breaking hours grinding grains (*ragi* and rice) now have this machine to do it for them. Children, who go to school, are also able to study in the evening hours. Each family contributes a sum of 20 rupees (around 40 US cents) each month towards the maintenance of the power plant.

Additionally, ten acres of land around the village is forest land which the people protect – no trees are cut here. They even manage to grow some fruit trees. A technology that improves the quality of life, while at the same time being earth-friendly, is sustainable. According to Larry Rasmussen,

> There are technical solutions to eco-social problems. They must be vigorously pursued. We will need all the earth-friendly technologies we can muster. At the same time, and several planes deeper, appropriate technology may not even be conceived, much less pursued, if reigning world-views (or "cosmologies") are haywire. Technologies express cultures. Ways of doing things reflect ways of seeing things.[29]

This is the India of today – a land of contradictions. India, a country where ecological history and the present degeneration of the environment intersect, placing the sub-continent on a precarious ledge with what looks like limited choices for greening itself – it seems like it has all gone too far. Is India beyond redemption and grace? This is also the India that embraces within its body the wisdom of Indigenous peoples and Dalit communities and particularly of women of those communities, who hold in their hands traditions of prudent care of the earth. How does the local reality link with the global? The use and abuse of water is taken now as a case study to describe this.

2. The Struggle for Water

Surrounded by forests,
protected by the rivers,
I have been born
in such a wonderful land.
There is gold and silver
And precious metals in this earth
I have been born
in such a wonderful land.
Yes, I have been born
in such a wonderful land.

Strangers are coming here
taking over our lakes and rivers.
Our spirits won't like it,
if we let others take over this land.
No, our spirits won't like it,
if we let others take over this land.[1]

India's ecological history is closely linked with global economic processes. After India's independence in 1948, the government set in place the process of planned development, built on the back of Western science and technology. The foundations were laid for a vast public sector for developing the infrastructure for industrial growth. At the same time the government encouraged the Indian capitalist class to invest in industrial expansion, giving birth to the concept of a mixed socialist economy. History textbooks often refer to Jawaharlal Nehru, the first prime minister of independent India, as "the architect of *modern* India". His efforts were on combining Western science and technology with "development" but under the frame of a socialist pattern of society. The Nehruvian model of development provided the direction for the path India chose when she became free. The neo-liberal market economy that came several decades later within the new phase of globalization has merely continued on this way, even more aggressively.

The introduction of mega dams as a part of the development process began right after independence. Nehru called the dams the "temples of modern India". He later regretted this statement,[2] but he had set in process a development paradigm from which there is no turning back. It has been assumed that big dams will deliver the people of India from hunger and poverty. Today, India is said to have 3600 big dams – 3300 of them were built after Nehru set India on this path. Another 695 big dams are under construction. This means that 40 percent of all big dams in the world are being built in India, in spite of the fact that one-fifth of the population of India does not have safe drinking water and two-thirds lack basic sanitation.[3] The damming of rivers, however, has lead to the destruction of peoples, their livelihood, their cultures and their lives. It can be callous, brutal and violent.

Women, and particularly Indigenous and Dalit women, in the Indian context, suffer the most when drinking-water resources become scarce. Women in the rural parts of India and in urban poor settlements, who had little access to water anyway, will now have less or, in some cases, none. It has other even more serious consequences on the lives of women. In one state in north India, it is said that the growing hardship of young women's lives due to ecological degradation has actually increased the number of suicides among them in recent years. "Their inability to obtain adequate quantities of water, fodder and fuel causes tensions with their mothers-in-law (in whose youth forests were plentiful) and soil erosion has compounded the difficulty of producing enough grain for subsistence in a region of high male out-migration."[4]

In the case of the Narmada project, referred to in the last chapter, the massive peoples' movements did manage to drive out the World Bank, yet this meant that the Bank and the International Monetary Fund have tightened their control on India by imposing even more conditions on other sectors of people's lives.

One area where the Bank and IMF have imposed the most worrying conditions is in ensuring *the privatization of water* – shifting control from the government to the corporate sector. Ironically, it is the World Bank that has predicted that by the year 2025 two-thirds of the world's population will not have access to clean drinking water! According to the United Nations Environmental Protection Organization, Asia will experience a shortage of clean water of up to 90 percent by 2050. Water has been defined as the "oil of the 21st century" – it is becoming a scarce resource and many predict that it could be the source of interstate conflicts. Is it any wonder then that transnational corporations have entered the fray to profit from this newly discovered treasure? In India the corporations that have entered to access this strategic good are Suez, Vivendi, Bechtel and Rheinisch-Westfalische Elektrizitatzwerke (RWE) – that now have been given the right to bottle water and sell it, as well as draw out the ground water for industrial purposes. They buy the water rights from small farmers, thus seriously reducing ground water reserves. The corporate sector, in close alliance with the Bank and the International Monetary Fund, has managed to turn this scarce resource from a "common" resource into a tradable, profitable and economic product to be owned, over-exploited, marketed and sold to whoever can pay for it. This basically denies millions of the poor in India the basic human right to clean water. The government has handed over its responsibility to the corporate sector, rather than focus attention and resources on looking for alternatives to ensure water availability for all, based on conservation and community control.

When water is privatized there is a false perception that the financial burden will shift from the government to the private sector and a more efficient system of water delivery will be set in place. In fact, it merely increases the price of water. For example in Bolivia, the privatization of the public water system as a condition for a World Bank loan doubled the price of water. Hundreds of thousands of Bolivians protested, this led to violent retaliation on the part of the state and many protestors were shot dead. Ironically, Bechtel, which is the parent company of the Bolivian subsidiary Aguas del Tunari, backed out and is now threatening to sue Bolivia for nearly $40 million! Bolivia, it must not be forgotten, is one of the poorest countries in South America. Additionally, the government's water department, which is a large public service sector in Bolivia that employs thousands of people, has laid off its workers. This is happening in other countries too. For example, in the Philippines half the original work-force in the metropolitan waterworks and sewerage system were laid off when this public works department was privatized.[5]

The international institutions

Between 2003 and 2004 the World Council of Churches initiated a process of *encounters with the Bretton Woods Institutions (the World Bank and the International Monetary Fund)* on their request for a dialogue. The intention of these organizations in inviting the dialogue was to encourage the WCC to make the churches more instrumental in some of their poverty reduction strategies. The WCC saw this as a moment to encounter these institutions on some of their policies, bringing to their attention the impact they are having on the third world. One of the issues addressed in these encounters was the question of the commodification of public goods and here water was identified as one of the most challenging questions of the day. Rogate Mshana, Tanzanian economist and the WCC staff person primarily responsible for the encounters, describes why this was identified as an issue for the dialogue:

The ecumenical movement maintains that water is a gift of God and a fundamental human right. It should remain under public responsibility and should not be traded. However, the World Bank, the IMF and corporations along with some governments favour the process of privatization following three methods – complete sale by governments of public water delivery and treatment systems to private corporations; long-term leases or concessions allowing corporations to take over the delivery of water services and collection of revenues; and corporations contracted by governments to manage water services for an administrative fee.

The World Bank and the IMF, in the name of promoting efficiency in water delivery, are forcing all these methods on the developing world. In all cases there have been successes and failures, leading to increased protests particularly in poor countries – Bolivia as already mentioned but also South Africa, Philippines, etc. Corporations see investment in water as a fast-growing business. It is estimated to be an annual billion-dollar industry, 40 percent of the size of the oil sector and one-third larger than pharmaceuticals. Most of these companies are the beneficiaries of the USD 20 billion lending of the World Bank to water supply projects over the last 12 years. A study of the International Centre for Public Integrity (ICPI) revealed that of the 276 World Bank water supply loans from 1990 to 2002 30 percent required privatization as a condition – the majority in the last five years. ICPI reports that an Argentine businessman earned a profit of USD 100 million on privatization. Bottled water is also a USD 33 billion annual business. So we have a scenario in the world of some who push for the marketing of water for profit, or water marketers, and others who are against it for moral and ethical reasons who are public service defenders.[6]

The ecumenical team that was present at the *13th session of the United Nations Commission on Sustainable Development,* in New York in April 2005, decided to focus their attention on water. In their statement, the ecumenical team reiterated that water is an essential gift of God and therefore must be protected for the whole of creation. Human beings are part of the creation and human society can only exist within the bio-system; its survival depends on the survival of the whole. Therefore, the care for the whole of creation must be the basis for the churches' engagement and action. As far as human society is concerned, our starting-point is that the access to water is a basic *human right*. It is a matter of justice and of social and political sustainability of any society that it must be ordered in such a way that all people can benefit from the gift of water. Therefore the team held that the protection and control of water resources is a central public *responsibility*. If water is a condition of life then water supply must be managed through structures representing all sectors of the population. Churches will call for comprehensive plans and measures to protect the availability of water. They asked that this right be enshrined in national constitutions.

States have the responsibility to create within their territory the best possible water conditions for all. This responsibility includes the protection of aquifers, measures against pollution and salinization, afforestation, etc. Public authorities are responsible for the adequate supply and the equitable distribution of water.

Water must not be treated as a *commercial good* or a commodity of trade. An essential good, it should not be subject to the rules of profit-making. Increasingly becoming a scarce good, it must be used sparingly. Water must be placed under public responsibility to guarantee access for all, including the impoverished sectors of society who do not have the purchasing power. This requires that water be protected as a public good belonging to humanity and all life. There is a pressing need to prevent water from being made into a commodity and degraded to a tradable good, so as to ensure that the human right to water takes precedence over international trade agreements (e.g. WTO). The team also urged that to the largest degree possible responsibility for the management and distribution of water should be placed in the hands of the *communities depending on it.* The principle of subsidiarity is essential for the maintenance and protection of water resources. Churches and church agencies will therefore consistently support and encourage the control of water resources by local communities. The team also recognized that water issues transcend national borders and therefore solutions can only be found through international solidarity, underlining that as water becomes scarce it can easily become a source of conflict. To preserve water resources, conflict-prevention is essential.[7] This has led to a global movement for the protection of water sources, and women have been central here.

Feminism

This being the case, it is important to review briefly the response of the women's movement and the eco-feminist movement to develop a theoretical framework for this engagement of women.

Feminist theory grew out of women's experiences of suffering and exclusion but also out of movements of survival and resistance. Women sought not just for new answers but for the formulation of new questions to understand systems of injustice in our world. The eco-feminist movement grew out of the feminist movement, and therefore some remarks about the women's movement itself are relevant here.

The word "feminism" was first used in Europe and North America in the late 1960s as a second stage in the earlier women's movements for emancipation. This second phase of the women's movement exposed the predicaments of a patriarchal world order and raised awareness of the disastrous affects of the traditional dualisms such as that between woman/nature and man/intellect. The impact of a male-dominated society was exposed and women began to organize themselves separately, as women, so as to give voice and political backing for their own interests – not necessarily as movements against men, but as expressions of women's longings for a new world of justice. Sexism was recognized as a category of discrimination, as was classism and racism.[8]

Feminism as a political ideology came to India only in the late 1970s. But women began to organize against oppression and patriarchal domination at the beginning of the 19th century. At that stage women's movements linked patriarchal oppression with imperialism and colonialism. While they did not call themselves "feminist" they were concerned with the liberation of women which went hand in hand with national liberation. There was no hierarchy of oppression within the struggles. From the outset, patriarchy was seen as linked with other structures of oppression. The issue of women's right to vote and political participation was raised as early as 1919 (but was rejected by the British – how could they allow this in India when women in Britain did not get the vote till 1928). In 1927 the All India Women's Conference was set up to discuss the issue of education for women and girls, but soon took up issues of *purdah* (veiling of women) and child-marriage. It was asserted that these questions could not be separated from the struggle for freedom from colonial rule. Women joined the Indian National Congress committee, took part in the Mahatma Gandhi-led civil disobedience movement and were prominent in the communist party as well as in revolutionary movements based on armed struggle.

Gandhi mobilized women in an unprecedented way. He associated "femininity" with spiritual and moral courage. He stressed women's superior capacity for suffering and self-sacrifice. He also insisted on absolute autonomy for women in the family and society. But though he exhorted women to be politically active, he seemed also to link their activism to their traditional roles and what he saw as the essential spirituality of women.

Additionally, around this time, women became involved and played a prominent role in the workers' movements and were active in the peasant revolt in Telengana. Apart from this, women began discussing how family, caste and community – which are key elements of patriarchal social organization in India – are instruments of control of women. Religion, particularly in minority communities – Christianity and Islam – had played a pivotal role in domesticating women and discouraging them from political engagement (there have been some significant examples of women from these communities breaking the lines of control).

From the 1960s there was another wave of the women's movement, with their engagement in political struggles – with the mass organization of women in consumer protection movements and women workers' movements. Their efforts in the land reform movement, however, ended with little land coming into their own hands.

It was in the 1970s that the autonomous women's movements came about. Feminism accused left parties and trade unions of being as patriarchal as the rest of society. The issues of dowry and rape mobilized women on a national scale. It was at this phase of the movement that links were established with a range of issues – work, environment, ecology, Dalit women's rights, civil and legal rights, reproductive rights, women's health, etc.

Unfortunately, since then there has been a co-option of some women's groups by the government with the "empowerment of women" as a rallying slogan – geared basically towards women's literacy as well as population control. The other concern is the "NGO-ization" of some groups and funding by international agencies. Nivedita Menon criticizes this external interference. There is

> danger of co-option: the compulsions of taking up and "successfully" completing specific projects has meant that there is hardly any serious thought given to what constitutes "feminism". It is as if these agencies have a clear understanding of what feminism is, and the groups funded by them only need to apply it to specific instances. Thus, autonomous women's groups which began as an attempt to create spaces outside the orthodoxies of party women's wings are now far from autonomous of the compulsions of getting and retaining funding.[9]

But it is important to note that the women's movement in India has played a pivotal political role in raising the profile of women's resistance.

Feminism is now a movement to contend with all over the world. Women in each context have expanded and defined feminism. Amrita Basu, an Asian feminist living in the US, introduces a collection of articles by women describing their contributions to feminism in many parts of the world. The book makes fascinating reading because it debunks the "sweeping generalizations about commonalties among women across the globe". Basu holds that "such generalizations aggravate tensions not only along North-South lines but also along lines of cleavage, including class, race and sexual orientation". She continues that

> paradoxically, the very attempt to universalize feminism makes it more exclusionary. The equation of feminism with movements organized by women autonomously from male-dominated organizations excludes many forms of activism within the context of democracy, nationalist and human-rights struggles in which women ultimately take up questions of gender inequality even if this is not their initial objective.[10]

Laura E. Donaldson, a Native American social scientist, believes that the impact of colonialism needs to be included in definitions of feminism. She attempts to

> counter white feminism's imperialist tendency to dive deep and surface with a single hermeneutic truth... white feminism's "discursive" colonization of the "third-world" woman... Many feminist discussions overlook the material specificity of gender and assign women's place within gender ideology according to the machinations of an a-historical patriarchy. If Marxism ignores the gender-saturated nature of all class-relations, then feminism ignores the racially saturated nature of all gender relations.[11]

African-American womanist theoretician Bell Hooks calls for a new approach that would recognize how many forces divide women – she particularly draws attention to racism, classism and homophobia, which divide women from one another:

> Splintering into different political factions and special interest groups has erected unnecessary barriers to sisterhood that could easily be eliminated. Special interest groups lead women to believe that only socialist feminists should be concerned about class; that only lesbian feminists should be concerned about the oppression of lesbians and gay men; that only black women or other women of colour should be concerned about racism. Every woman can stand in political opposition to sexist, racist, heterosexist and classist oppression... When we show our concern for the collective, we strengthen our solidarity.[12]

The challenge is how we as women, globally, are going to overcome these divides among us and the resultant inadequate ways in which we have organized ourselves and have developed feminist theory. It is imperative and good that we define our struggles, and diverse identities through which we participate in struggles, in the most appropriate ways to our contexts. However, it is not helpful if this requires us to divide ourselves and fault each other's positions. After all, we are all as women in the process of developing alternative political paradigms for the transformation of our societies and of our unjust world.

Feminist theory has to become more inclusive, simply because of its revolutionary potential for all women. We need this inclusive approach in the context of the political vacuum created by globalization and the unipolar world we live in. Feminism's power (however we name it in our own contexts) as a political, social and cultural alternative paradigm cannot be underestimated. It is of critical importance to all women and to third-world women in particular, at the time when so many efforts are made to devalue the struggles of women in the third world, by men in our societies. We are told we are being reductionist and elitist when we speak up for women. Mercy Oduyoye, for example, speaks of how "African men insisted that liberation as applied to African woman was a foreign importation. Some even called it an imperialist trap that would do Africa no good."[13] We are told that poverty, national liberation, racism etc. must come first and that we betray third-world cultures when we speak on issues related to women. It is urgent therefore for us to hold together a movement that would challenge patriarchy, its violent attitudes and practices in dealing with women as well as its deep links with colonialism, neo-colonialism and the cultural values it has legitimized and promoted. Such a movement would also challenge an economic framework and a development paradigm that is accompanied by the exclusion of life for millions of people and the profligate use of the gifts of the earth.

The eco-feminist movement

Out of the women's movement the eco-feminist movement emerged in the 1970s as a response to the increasing consciousness of the connections between women and their commitment to the protection of creation. The French writer Francoise d'Eaubonne coined the term *eco-feminisme* in 1974. She called on women to lead an ecological revolution to save the planet. It was expected that such an ecological movement would entail new gender relations between women and men and between humans and nature.[14] It was a direct challenge to the excessive anthropocentrism of social justice movements, including the women's movement, which had been strong in critiquing the androcentric character of societies but had not been strong enough in recognizing human destructiveness in relating with the earth.

There are many ways in which women have defined eco-feminism, each from their own contexts and it is important to look at these and to recognize the commonality and differences among women. Rosemary Radford Ruether acknowledges the differences between how women of Europe and North America and women of Asia, Africa and Latin America relate with creation. In her estimation, "many essentialist or matricentric Northern eco-feminists fail to make real connections between their own reality as privileged women and racism, classism, and impoverishment of nature".[15] She does commend the contributions of eco-feminists of the North

> in analyzing the connection of women and nature as expressions of an ideology and a socio-economic system by the male elite. Many have also been interested in how to hold to this historical cultural connection of women and nature as a positive relation by which women can stand in solidarity with exploited nature, resist the violence done to nature and to themselves and become healers of nature.[16]

However, Radford Ruether warns that the psycho-spiritual reconnecting of women's bodies and nature can become a recreational self-indulgence if

> the healing of our bodies and our imaginations as Euro-Americans is not connected concretely with the following realities of over-consumption and waste: the top 20 percent of the world's human population enjoys 82 percent of the wealth while the other 80 percent scrapes along with 18 percent; and the poorest 20 percent of the world's people, over a *billion* people – disproportionately women and children – starve and die early from poisoned waters, soil and air. A Northern eco-feminism that is not primarily a cultural escapism for an affluent elite must make concrete connections with women at the bottom of the social-economic system.[17]

One vital difference therefore between first-world and third-world eco-feminism is the concern about intentionally created poverty and wealth. Women in the third world see the poverty that afflicts whole communities (particularly women and children) and land as the base line for understanding domination of women and of nature. Additionally, women of these regions are trying to recover patterns of spirituality that connect them to their indigenous roots – a past that is still present in the lives of communities, as women care for the earth. To Radford Ruether, this past "has been broken and silenced by colonialism and Christianization, but is still present in the contemporary Indigenous people of one's own land, descendants of one's own Indigenous ancestors, or even as customs with which the woman writer herself grew up in her earlier years".[18]

She contends that an eco-feminist goes "beneath the cultural-symbolic level and explores the socio-economic underpinnings of how the domination of women's bodies and women's work connects with the exploitation of land and sources of labour and wealth".[19] She asks a series of questions to define her own understanding of eco-feminism: Have women been colonized by patriarchy? Do women's bodies and labour function as the invisible substructure for the extraction of wealth? How does the positioning of women as care-takers in the family make this work inferior? And how does this identify women with the non-human world that is also given an inferior status?

Vandana Shiva, who has been one of the most vocal eco-feminists in India, bases her work on the conviction that women are victims of the violence of patriarchal forms of development. Therefore women have risen against it to protect nature and preserve their survival and sustenance. She describes how Indian women who have been in the forefront of ecological struggles to conserve forests, land and water have challenged "the Western concept of nature as an object of exploitation and have protected her as Prakriti, the living force that supports life... the feminine principle from which all life arises".[20]

However, one must avoid essentialism here. There is danger in speaking of all women, whether we speak of the first world or of all third world, as one category. We are not. Essentialism tends to make some women's historical subordination to men (and to other women, I must add) seem like a natural fact rather than as a cultural and even political product.[21] For instance in the first world there are deeply marked divisions of race and class and ignoring this would not do justice to the women there. Shamara Shantu Riley, an African-American eco-womanist, believes that the problem lies in the fact that

> many eco-feminists, when analyzing the links between human relations and ecological degradation, give primacy to gender and thus fail to thoroughly incorporate (as opposed to mere tokenism) the historical links between classism, white supremacy and environmental degradation, in their perspectives. For instance, they often don't address the fact that, in nations where such variables as ethnicity and class are a central organizing principle of society, many women are not only viewed in opposition to men under dualism, but also to other women... Unlike most white women, black women are not limited to issues defined by their femaleness but are rather often limited to questions raised about our very humanity.[22]

What she says in the context of African-American women in the US reads the same for India, too. We have to acknowledge our deep divisions and the fact that for many Indigenous and Dalit women in India destruction of the environment is destruction of life itself. There is a different world-view, a different analysis and definitely their own traditional resources with which third-world women survive. Bina Agarwal wonders whether there is a need to use an alternative formulation that would embrace this experience of third-world women. She suggests the term "feminist environmentalism" rather than the more commonly used term "ecofeminism".[23]

Agarwal critiques Vandana Shiva for conflating all third-world women into one category, and for making the same mistake as white eco-feminists of not differentiating "between women of different classes, castes, races, ecological zones and so on".[24] Agarwal also faults Shiva for failing to "recognize the coexistence of several ideological strands, given India's ethnic and religious diversity".[25] She contests Shiva's use of the "feminine principle as the guiding idea in Indian philosophical discourse", which "in fact relates to the Hindu discourse alone and cannot be seen as applicable for Indians of all religious persuasions".[26]

However, we also have to acknowledge "a positive form of the essentialist argument",[27] which women such as Narango embody. This is to underline that women can bring new ways of acting, new insights, new values and commitments into the ways they live in community, and in this context in the ways they live with the earth. Serene Jones makes a helpful distinction between an essentialist/universalist stance of some feminists, on the one hand, which she defines as a "constructivist" position, and those feminists who show how "thick essentialist stones are made not from solid rock but from the humanly constructed porous material of culture".[28] She suggests a middle way between these two positions which she defines as "strategic essentialism" for which feminist theologians would opt, i.e. of recognizing the value of some essentialist characteristics so as to find common ground for women to act collectively (and even globally) for social change.[29]

In the final analysis, it is not the labelling of different definitions of feminist contributions that matter, but to emphasize that from our specific experience as Indian women something new can be offered to transform injustice in our world. In India, as in other third-world countries, but also among under-privileged communities in the first world, it is poor women who have been most affected by environmental destruction. Additionally, it is women most affected by the destruction of the earth who are most active in the movements to protect the earth. This is because they are defending their own survival when they struggle for the survival of the earth. We will need to acknowledge the existence of many "eco-feminisms" in our world – all pioneered by women passionately committed to justice and dignity for women and for all of creation. As Ivone Gebara suggests,

> the term "ecofeminism" may not survive for long, but that is of no importance whatsoever. The important thing is that the values embodied in this vision be respected, along with their local articulations. The important thing is that the affirmation that we are all one and the same Sacred Body in multiple and diverse expressions, an affirmation that arises from our own experience, be allowed to stand and serve as the basis for the diversity of our reflections.[30]

Gebara describes the energy that sustains eco-feminism as an alternative value that women offer inspired by an "energy flow that brings about political and cultural change and gets us moving, excites our minds, revives our imaginations and unleashes our questions".[31]

Therefore, women *challenge not only androcentrism but also anthropocentrism: the earth as central in women's analysis*. The Christian tradition and more particularly feminist theology does contain the foundations for a liberatory ethic that would challenge all forms of oppression – for all of humanity and for the earth. Letty Russell underlines that feminist theology "reaches for a new mode of relationship: neither a hierarchical model that diminishes the potential of the 'other' nor an 'equality' defined by a ruling norm drawn from the dominant group, but rather a mutuality that allows us to affirm different ways of being".[32] She continues, "in rejecting androcentrism (males as norms of humanity) women must also criticize all other forms of chauvinism: making white Westerners the norm of humanity, making Christians the norm of humanity; making privileged classes the norm of humanity".[33] She goes a step further when she refers to the foundations of an eco-feminist theology, challenging the anthropocentrism of traditional theology. Russell believes that feminist theology must "also criticize humanocentrism: making humans the norm and "crown" of creation in a way that diminishes other beings in the community of creation".[34] This suggests an epistemological shift that renders to the earth its integrity and is open to learn from the wisdom of the earth.

Additionally women underline an *ethic of eco-justice as the frame of analysis* as both the poor and the earth cry out for justice. Nature can be seen as the new poor, "not the poor that crowds out the human poor, but the 'also' poor (referring to the earth); and as such it demands our attention and care".[35] This requires political engagement to transform the injustice that is done both to the earth and to the poor. Leonardo Boff speaks of social ecology as the way in which social and economic systems interact with the natural ecosystem, and "since the human race is part of the environment, social injustice goes hand-in-hand with ecological injustice".[36] Larry Rasmussen too defines the earth's distress as socio-ecological. In other words the rights attributed to the earth include the rights of all of humankind (not just some) to also live and survive. He underlines that it is not possible to see "'humanity' as some nebulous whole... but for varied human beings who presently occupy different strata in domestic and world social orders".[37] Our commitment to the earth and to peoples of the earth needs be held together in one frame.

An ethic of care

There is also an *ethic of care* and therefore the search for *a caring economy* as an alternative that women offer. In recent times the World Council of Churches has been engaged in the development of alternatives to economic globalization. Women have made significant contributions to this work. Athena Peralta from the Philippines, a feminist social scientist who has developed this work, emphasizes that "the foremost methodological principle in economic analyses is based on the understanding that unpaid social reproductive or caring labour – which is essentially about the maintenance of human life outside of the market – is a vital part of any economic system. That is, the economy is much bigger than the production, distribution and consumption of goods and services that can be sold in markets."[38] She analyzes how women's negative experiences with economic globalization are rooted in the material and moral devaluing of women's productive and domestic labour. "Feminist economists have been advocating for, among others, the inclusion and visibility of the care economy in all national income accounts and the factoring in of care work in all economic models and analyses."[39]

In discussing an ethic of care we have so much to learn from Indigenous women and Dalit women, and the depth of their ecological wisdom that comes from the prudent care with which they have lived with creation. This is not to legitimize the language of biological determinism that presumes some kind of inherent link between women and nature. However, the affirmation made by Narango, the Indigenous woman in Koraput, that "there is a relationship between the woman and the land" and that the "earth is like our mother, like a mother who cares for her children selflessly" emphasizes a relational character with the land. Narango also spoke of how "we as women who also go through the same processes of birthing and caring need to also nurture the earth".

Feminists, both social scientists and theologians, have lifted up the ethic of care based on "women's relational sense of self".[40] In other words when women acknowledge their interdependence as caring individuals they assert their identity on their own terms. Pamela Brubaker describes this poignantly:

> I think of people with hearts that are tender, warm, caring, passionate, strong, brave; of people who hearten each other in the face of heartbreaking realities; of many hearts beating with the heart of the universe. "Heart" is a good symbol for some of the distinctive contributions that feminist ethics brings to an ethic for just and sustainable community: emotion, relationality and care. Stout hearts, clear eyes, open ears, dirty hands – all are essential for our common task.[41]

For an Indigenous woman such as Narango, political engagement is a natural corollary to the ethic of care.

Narango sees the life-giving earth as her mother, and claims motherhood as a life-giving quality that she feels honoured to embody as she engages in political action for a healed earth. This inspires theological reflections on the image of the earth as the body of God and as mother. This will be addressed later in this book.

The search for *a new feminist epistemology* is rooted in the knowledge systems of women who have lived in prudent relationship to the earth and who engage in resisting projects of "development" that threaten to destroy that relationship. It is based on a commitment to transform hierarchical structures of power and injustice. The transformation of unjust structures is critical because traditional understandings of society emerge out of and are framed by centres of abusive power. Feminist epistemology is based on a desire to seek alternatives that are based on eco-justice and are grounded in an ethic of care. The question to be asked is whether they are "merely new topics to be reflected on and integrated into our traditional ways of thinking, or will dealing with them lead us to work at modifying the very models we use to think about the world?"[42] Brazilian feminist theologian Ivone Gebara's critique is that what we now call "knowing" is limited to "a particular perspective on reality, itself determined by a specific group responsible for formulating this perspective".[43] Eco-feminists reject traditional ways of knowing as being both androcentric and anthropocentric and therefore limited in their scope. What is called for is an alternative epistemology i.e. "to construct new styles of knowing that are intimately related to our new cosmologies".[44] Gebara calls for an overcoming of dualistic and hierarchical ways of knowing and to break out of "Euro-centred" controls of our knowing and "of the various forms of imperialist 'corner-on-the-truth' attitudes upheld by the Western world".[45]

To eco-feminists it is the wisdom and knowledge of the poor, of Indigenous women, of Dalit women that has over the centuries been systematically ignored and suppressed that must be brought centre-stage. This is based on an understanding that in such knowledge we will find resources to reverse the ecological destruction that has been caused by dominant ways of knowing and the so-called scientific forms of enquiry. This new epistemology demands new ethical judgments on what is good, just and sustainable.

Exploring the resistance movements of Indigenous women in the Utharkhand region of the Himalayas, Vandana Shiva concludes that

> the intellectual heritage of ecological survival lies with those who are experts in survival. They have the knowledge and experience to extricate us from the ecological cul-de-sac that the Western masculinist mind has manoeuvred us into. And while third-world women have privileged access to survival expertise, their knowledge is inclusive, not exclusive. The ecological categories with which they think and act can become the categories of liberation for all, for men as well as for women, for the West as well as for the non-West, for the human as well as the non-human elements of the earth.[46]

With this as the backdrop, women have developed an alternative theological vision, with "motherhood" as a theological value that underlines both relationality and a feminist ethic of care. Motherhood in Indian society is a strong notion of interdependence and of life-sustaining courage and could be defining for humanity's inextricable bond with creation and the bond between human beings, for the healing of the earth. However, the concept of motherhood has to be "rescued" from its patriarchal overtones. It requires the deconstruction of traditional understandings of the concept of motherhood and the reconstruction of new meanings so as to develop a new resource to inspire both a caring attitude and an understanding of political engagement for environmental care. The women's movement has been cautious in reclaiming motherhood, because of the ways in which it has been used to keep women in subjugation and women theologians in India and elsewhere warn that this needs to be carefully done as it has the potential to be romanticized and misread – they know what the patriarchal family structure has done to motherhood.

The warning of women theologians is well placed. Feminist scholarship cannot ignore the fact that the creative and selfless love of women and their sexuality has been idealized and abused to restrict women's time, space and movement. It is necessary to debunk patriarchy's appropriation of motherhood and the ways in which the rights and dignity of women in India and elsewhere have been trampled on so as to control their sexuality and creativity. This gift of women – their productive and reproductive capacity – has been exploited, "used", and women have been sold as symbols of sexuality, or more often they have been exploited as unpaid labour in the free-market project of economic growth. Women's sexuality has also been exploited for the procreation of children so as to maintain male patriarchal lineage. Therefore, a woman who is unable to bear children or opts not to do so is treated as an aberration facing abuse and discrimination in many contexts.

The sexuality, fertility and creative power of women and their roles as mothers must be reclaimed from the distortions and control of patriarchy, because there is more to motherhood than its traditional interpretations. Motherhood is not just a biological role, in India it is a strong symbol of nurture and care. Whether women are biological mothers or not they are conferred with titles such as *amma* and *ma* by their communities (not just within the confines of their immediate biological families), and often appropriate the privileges and responsibilities that go with it. Additionally, we have a heritage of goddesses in pre-Aryan and in other religious traditions most often represented as virgin, mother and fertility symbol. Mothers therefore represent creativity, regeneration and sustenance, affirming women's sexuality and bodies as symbols of life and the sustainability of communities.

In recent years, several women theologians have attempted to reclaim the power of motherhood and the potential it offers for more earth caring attitudes. Gabriele Dietrich drawing on the experience of fisher-folk women and women in the unorganized sector of workers in urban poor settlements in India, shows how motherhood provides a symbolic and practical link between the production of life and subsistence production. She too recognizes how "the sexual division of labour between patriarchal technological, political and economic structures, and the privatized pursuits of mothering and nurturing, lies at the root of the ongoing ecological destruction". She goes on to affirm,

> If we recognize God as a mother, then motherhood and nurture must also be the guiding principle for the reorganization of economic and political structures. Motherhood, the continued blessing over the good creation, follows its own unorthodox ways. It is not tied to the confines of patriarchal society. Yet, it must be fully unbound only if the shackles are broken.[47]

The reclaiming of motherhood, as an alternative theological ethic, cannot therefore be an esoteric exercise; neither is it tinged with romanticism. It is a pragmatic and practical concern symbolic of resilience and resistance. It is situated in the everyday struggles, particularly of women, for access to clean water, clean air, fuel, food and fodder. As this challenges "essentialist" connections between women and nature as mentioned earlier. Women are the ones engaged in the "production of survival" of themselves and of their families – and therefore have a vested interest in protecting the earth and its resources. It is out of this survival imperative that traditions of prudence have evolved and continue to exist as resistance movements against the dominant development paradigm and economic growth. The earth is in need of our mothering.

Shamara Shantu Riley speaks of the traditions of prudence of African women and draws attention to these women's capacity to care for the earth, but also of their political activism in environmental movements describing them as "Afro-American eco-motherists". "Motherists" have been defined as women who, for various reasons, "identify themselves not as feminists but as militant mothers fighting together for survival".[48] Riley continues:

> Motherism usually arises when men are absent or in times of crisis, when the private role assigned to women under patri-

> archy makes it impossible for the collective to survive. Since they are faced with the dictates of traditional work but face a lack of resources in which to fulfil their socially prescribed role, motherists become a political force.[49]

The ethic of care found in motherhood definitely needs further exploration and discussion among women so that we can together discover the power of women to create life-sustaining alternatives to the present systems of power, which are dangerously on the brink of destroying the earth and its peoples. Women through their traditions of prudence and their actions of resistance reveal a power that cannot be ignored.

As the poem at the opening of this chapter shows, the Indigenous peoples who faced displacement because of the Subarnarekha dam project took an oath "that we will always protect our land and rivers". Words of courage and even of foolishness against the might of those who have economic, political and even military power to suppress any movement that stands in the way of their "development" project! To the people this often means death – therefore they clamour for alternatives, sometimes facing violence in the hands of those with power. The question we need to ask is why the courage and commitment of eco-system peoples, who are determined to protect the earth, have not been able adequately to influence the church and the ecumenical movement? Why is their wisdom still only on the edges of our theological reflections?

3. Christianity as an Earth Faith

The threads binding society
Are breaking.
Our brothers and sisters
Are stumbling in darkness.
Our community is falling apart.

Let's knit it up
Let's plait it together again![1]

The questions to be addressed are straightforward. How can we listen to the earth and the children of the earth so as to deconstruct some traditional theological understandings that have contributed to the destructive ways in which we have lived with the earth? How can the churches and the ecumenical movement reconstruct a new theological vision inspired by traditions of prudence and the integrity of creation? There is no doubt that the ecumenical movement has come some way, because in 1988 at a meeting of the World Council of Churches in Granvollen, Norway, it was said,

> For the sake of all creation, theology must begin with creation. We have learnt that true peace can only be realized through the establishment of justice, and that peace flows naturally out of justice, so now we must begin to learn that justice and then peace flow naturally out of a deep respect for creation.[2]

In the WCC definition of "the integrity of creation" there is both a "social aspect" and an "ecological aspect". "The integrity of creation forbids division of human from otherkind or humans from one another",[3] and "the integrity of creation has a social aspect which we recognize as peace with justice, and an ecological aspect which we recognize in the self-renewing, sustainable character of natural eco-systems".[4]

The question to be asked is whether Christianity, more specifically Protestant Christianity, is ambivalent about earth loyalties? There is some difference of opinion here, and different positions.[5] What we need to do urgently is to discover the resources within Protestant Christianity to counter some of the mistakes made in Christianity's history. For instance, there are records of how the missionary movement had undermined the value attached to the earth and to its sacredness by Indigenous and other eco-system peoples.

In recent times, theologians have begun to interrogate this history and some elements of Christianity and other religions that subvert environmental goals. Christianity has been singled out in this respect and Lynn White Jr's seminal article dealing with this subject, for instance, points out that

> In Antiquity every tree, every spring, every stream, every hill had its own genius loci, its guardian spirit... Before one cut a tree, mined a mountain, or dammed a brook, it was important to placate the spirit in charge of that particular situation and to keep it placated. By destroying pagan animism, Christianity made it possible to exploit nature in a mood of indifference to the feelings of natural objects.[6]

Theologian Mary Grey borrows Thomas Berry's phrase "turn from the earth"[7] to describe the moment when Jewish and Christian traditions left the earth behind. She says it was when Greek humanism combined with biblical traditions and gave ascendancy to an anthropocentric view of the universe. The Bible, regrettably, seemed to be playing a role in "encouraging human greed". The sacred texts were "read in a way that stimulates and condones anthropocentrism".[8] However, today it is increasingly recognized that such a negative potential of religions must be

> brought to consciousness and examined courageously, and meditated upon with all honesty, in dialogue with the wider community of thinkers, secular and religious, who are concerned about the ecological question. Sweeping them under the rug will not do, if they are indeed antithetic to ecological awareness, for their influence is bound to remain in force, generating consequences, in the cultures that support them... the *negative* outcomes of religious teachings that can be used to rationalize environmental neglect are probably greater than the *positive* influence of those that encourage conservation and protection.[9]

In the face of the large-scale environmental damage in our world, the urgency of this task cannot be underestimated. As a corollary to this, there is a need to review the positions taken by the ecumenical movement to see whether its positions too have been influenced unduly by the ambivalence of Protestant theology. Additionally, we need to assess whether the epistemologies of women and other groups on the edges of the church influence ecumenical social thought? Has ecumenical theology remained deeply entrenched in a Euro-centric, patriarchal and anthropocentric world-view?

It is important to heed what environmentalists of all faith traditions are saying and the last decades have thankfully seen a growing number of theologians reflecting from an ecological perspective. However, there is an element that is not strong enough, or is sometimes missing altogether, in the writings of many environmental theologians who fail to stress the integral relation between social and environmental justice. There seems to be reluctance to relate with the political dimension of history, with regards to the conquest of nature and of the earth. These theologians do not address questions of unequal power relations in our world and the way this impacts the earth. As Larry Rasmussen reminds us, our work will be incomplete if we do not recognize that we have to address at one and the same time the three great instabilities of injustice, un-peace and creation's disintegration.[10]

This is particularly important in the context of Christianity's historical role. Colonialism and the desire to "develop" nations that had led to the conquest and occupation and the extraction of resources/wealth of colonized nations, was closely linked to a particular understanding of Christian theology. Such an ideology persists till today, and it is therefore urgent for Christianity to address these questions.

Challenges to Christian theology

Suspicion is often caste on monotheistic religions, such as Christianity, and the role they have played in attitudes to the earth. Larry Rasmussen believes that Christians are stuck in an awkward space between two worlds just now: between the familiar world – the world we thought we trusted and depended on, a world we believed was governed by what we considered to be universal principles and values, and another world that challenges such a world-view.[11] We now hear new voices of hope from women, from Indigenous peoples of the world, from subaltern groups such as the Dalits and from the earth itself. These are strangely new voices, but they have to be heeded. There is a call for a major paradigm shift, a journey into the unknown and unfamiliar. This is a demand to be attentive to history, the place and the memories that go with it and the experiences that give it and the community identity.

Referring to the serious eco-crisis we face and the danger of religion's inability to respond, Daniel Maguire warns, "If current trends continue, *we* will not. And that is qualitatively and epochally true. If religion does not speak to [this], it is an obsolete distraction."[12] Is Christianity becoming an obsolete distraction? What do we do in order to ensure that Christianity "might yet become an earth faith"?[13] Rasmussen writes,

> Most of Christianity, for example, has been human-centred and male-centred in conception and leadership. It has been dysfunctionally and destructively dualistic on many forms, including the fateful splitting of spirit from matter, mind from body, and humanity from the rest of nature... From its own scriptures onwards, it has been deeply ambivalent about the body and sensuality. Much of it has contributed mightily to modernity, largely supporting an industrial, technological and urban world deeply at odds with the rest of the planet.[14]

Eco-feminist theologians have been critical of Christianity because of the dualisms and feminists trace this to Greek thought and Greek influences on Christianity. Some feminists would blame early modern thinkers such as Descartes and Newton for the rational mode of analysis and the ways in which this transformed our relationship to the earth. They critique the language that assumes that the natural world can also be quantified, made "objective", and can be studied exhaustively by the inductive, empirical method. They call for a shift in our consciousness so as to develop new resources to care for the earth out of ancient wisdoms. Sallie McFague, for instance, gives the example of the Navajo for whom the "beauty way" is "a spiritual invocation of the order of the exterior universe" which is understood to possess an integrity that is unimpeachable and beyond human analysis.[15] Feminist theologians too call for this new way.

The ecumenical movement has debated deeply some aspects of Christianity that have contributed to our ambivalent attitude to the earth. First, the fact that the Bible is not always clear on where it stands in relation to creation; and second, that some fundamentals of Christian theology have only reinforced this exploitative attitude to the earth.

Perhaps the most discussed verses in the Bible relating to ecology are the two accounts of creation in Genesis, i.e. the records in chapters 1 and 2. Generally, Genesis 2 is treated as the more fundamental, in part because it is the older version. It is definitely more palatable to liberation theologians and eco-theologians. Genesis 2:15, "The Lord God took the man and put him in the Garden of Eden to till it and keep it" (Revised Standard Version) has been translated in the New Revised Standard Version as "to work it and take care of it". This new translation places the human being in relationship to the rest of creation, as just one part of creation. We are reminded that we belong to the earth and live by it and our primary relationship is one of interdependence with the earth. Even God is portrayed as a divine farmer who cares for the life of the earth. God places human beings to work on the earth and supervises their work. God is seen as making Adam serve the soil, to make her green.[16] But in Genesis 1:28, the problems emerge. This text refers to the human empowered to "fill the earth and *subdue* it; and have *dominion...* over every living thing that moves upon the earth". The words "subdue" and "dominion" are problematic.

For most thoughtful Christians the *theology of dominion* is no longer normative, because they know of the destruction and oppression it has brought with it. Yet, regretfully, it remains the reigning axiom "where it counts most, *in prac-*

tice".[17] We still believe that the earth exists for us and that we can do with it what we will for the sake of our own good. It is this doctrine that was both at the heart of colonial expansion and continues to undergird distorted understandings of development. Larry Rasmussen points out that "both industrial and informational 'ecologies' hold these as the practical doctrine of their working cosmologies and sell their promises on the basis of them... Commerce masquerading as liberation is not the only surviving form of dominion theology, but it is the most prominent one."[18]

Once in a while this discussion comes up in the church and the ecumenical movement too, and is justified theologically. A theology of dominion was defended at the 1966 Geneva conference of the Church and Society department of the WCC entitled "Christians in the Technical and Social Revolutions of Our Time":

> The traditional Christian doctrine of creation is an obvious basis for the view that God acts in and upon nature. It teaches that nature is both to be dominated by man and to be offered to man's contemplation and awe... Nature is under both the providence of God and the mastery of men... We cannot and we must not speak of nature apart from human perception in the historical development of knowledge, since man gives meaning to nature; as such, he is the crown of creation. In this sense the comprehension of nature is theologically anthropocentric... They (men) can proceed with scientific and technical research and development without fear of being impious or guilty of desecration. It is this deification or desacralization of nature, which is one basic starting point of true science and of its results in technology.[19]

This conference spoke synonymously of stewardship and mastery. It was similar kind of language that persisted into the third assembly of the WCC in New Delhi in 1961. Here it was stated that, "The nature that scientists investigate is part of God's creation; the truth they discover is part of God's truth; the abilities they use are God-given. *The Christian should welcome scientific discoveries as new steps of man's dominion over nature.*"[20]

A hymn, inspired by Psalm 8, sung during regular Sunday worship services in some Protestant churches, also places human beings in a position of dominance:

> Yet you have made us less than gods
> Surpassing all but you
> With heart and mind with strength and will
> To search for what is true.
> Into our hands you've placed all things
> The earth, the sea, each place
> We're called to probe for secret gifts
> And venture into space.[21]

Such a theology has given to humanity unlimited power to explore earth, sea and even space – so as to colonize wherever human beings venture. Theologians have pointed out how the Christian concept of dominion has played a key role in legitimizing the way Western science has "taken control of" and manipulated creation to humanity's advantage. There are differences of opinion no doubt, and yet it is difficult to ignore the link between Christianity, science and technology, capitalism and how Greek philosophy had influenced this. Carolyn Merchant discerns these links in the European urge to "reinvent the whole earth in the image of the Garden of Eden".[22] This project was accompanied by the colonizing of the world, so as to make true the proposal of recovery of Paradise Lost (the lost Eden) in the Genesis account, or of dominion over all of the earth and all of creation.

> Aided by the Christian doctrine of redemption and the inventions of science, technology and capitalism ("arte and *industrie*"), the long-term goal of the recovery project has been to turn the earth itself into a vast cultivated garden... Modern Europeans added two components to the Christian recovery project – mechanistic science and *laissez-faire* capitalism – to create a grand master narrative of Enlightenment. Mechanistic science supplies the instrumental knowledge of reinventing the garden on earth.[23]

It is this logic that has also been the basis of the concept of development that was propagated after the second world war. Closely associated with the political freedom (from colonization) that Asian, African and Latin American nations achieved in this period, beginning with India in 1947, was the fascination of the newly independent states with Western technology and the marvels of Western science. Additionally, the cold war led to the two power blocs entering into competition to enlarge their sphere of ideological, political and economic influence. Both promoted the same form of industrial development, which had a similar impact on the earth and its survival. Mainstream theology has not addressed this enough nor emphasized the connections between the resource extracting nature of the present development paradigm and the theology of dominion. Perhaps this is because dominant theologies are not adequately influenced by liberation theologies. Post-colonial scholars as well as feminist theologians, liberation theologians and some other subaltern voices have begun such discussions – but this has been largely peripheral to theological reflections of the churches.

To the ecumenical movement, however, this has been a concern for some decades now. David J. Wellman[24] makes a useful collection of the statements and major discussions in the ecumenical movement, critiquing the concept of sustainable development and affirming the commitment to the concept of sustainable communities. Larry Rasmussen[25] has been one of the most influential ethicists in the ecumenical movement in recent times. He has challenged the assumptions implicit in the accepted notion of development and its impact on the sustainability of the earth.

The Protestant churches' commitment to development was linked to the mission of the church, with service to the poor or charity as a primary commitment. The grinding poverty around the world had moved the churches to diaconal action from their very foundations. The 1966 Geneva conference on Church and Society referred to earlier, for the first time, argued for systemic political and cultural transformation as against the traditional mission/charity approach of the churches. The strong presence and contributions of third-world churches was felt in the ecumenical movement and this contributed to this shift in understanding. But even then, some churches were of the opinion that the church's role is to focus on charity and relief and that they should not involve themselves in political engagement to challenge the global economic roots of poverty. So right from the outset two streams of thinking could be discerned within the ecumenical movement – one which spoke of reforms within the existing systems and the other that demanded more radical structural changes.[26]

Since its inception in 1948, the WCC has made statements against laissez-faire capitalism and the economic and social injustices in the international economic order. In more recent times (since the eighth assembly of the WCC in Harare, Zimbabwe, 1998), economic globalization has been strongly challenged. The terms and conditions of world trade, its administration by the World Trade Organization and its impact on the poor and on the earth receive special attention today. The Harare assembly referred to globalization as a "new form of domination", whose driving forces are economic powers which were described as being "as insidious as political colonizers". Harare pointed to the unequal distribution of power and to the increasing levels of poverty and exclusion. It criticized the role of global communication in fostering a "consumerist monoculture". The Harare assembly noted that the "global economic system is blind to its destructive social and ecological consequences".[27]

At all times, some theologians have been critical of the language of dominion. To post-colonial theologians, the word "dominion" could slide into a legitimization of imperial mastery that was part of church history in colonial times. This is because Western history was sometimes too closely aligned with "civilization" and "dominion". For example, in 1885 Congregational minister, Josiah Strong, proudly noted that the Anglo-Saxon has a "genius for colonizing", for "he excels all others in *pushing his way* into new countries". For Strong, the Anglo-Saxon was not only "divinely commissioned to be, in a peculiar sense, his brother's keeper, but as such was indeed his indisputable destiny".[28] This has legitimized the claim of Christianity for dominion over other religions, cultures and peoples. It is this same desire to dominate and build empires that we hear again today in the context of the so-called "war on terrorism and on evil" by what is perceived as a "Christian" United States (and implicitly in the name of a "Christian" God).

However, it is equally important to recognize that some Protestant biblical scholars do not understand the word "dominion" to mean "domination". They contend that Genesis 1:28 is not about hierarchy and anthropomorphism, concepts which environmentalists find repulsive. Some mainline and evangelical theologians perceive "the word to suggest service, servanthood and caring as modelled by Christ"[29] which is very different from dominion. Jurgen Moltmann, for one, believes that it is not the human who is the "crown of creation", but it is the sabbath. The creation story begins in verse 2 and is completed only with the sabbath, when God finishes the work begun.[30] Rosemary Radford Ruether too challenges the usually misunderstood concept of dominion in the Genesis text. She draws attention to the Lynn White Jr text mentioned earlier and writes,

> Environmentalists have criticized the idea of "dominion" given this collective Adam over the rest of creation as the prototype of both anthropocentric and exploitative use of the animals and plants by "man". There is not doubt that the account is anthropocentric. Although created last, the human is the crown of creation, given sovereignty over it.[31]

But to Radford Ruether sovereignty given to humans does not allow for an exploitative or destructive rule over the earth.

> Humans are not given ownership or possession of the earth, which remains "the Lord's". God, finally, is the one who possesses the earth as his creation. Humans are given usufruct of it. Their role is the secondary one of care for it as a royal steward, not as an owner who can do with it what he wills.[32]

The second theological dilemma is in the use of the word "stewardship". Radford Ruether qualifies her description of the stewardship model by using the word "usufruct" in her statement. The legal definition of "usufruct", as in Webster's dictionary, is the "right of using and enjoying the profits of an estate or other things belonging to another, without impairing the substance". Therefore here Radford Ruether accords to humans the secondary role "of care for it (creation) as its royal steward" – she underlines that "it is not as an owner who can do with it what he wills".[33] Stewardship has been the way in which we as human beings understand our responsibility to care for the earth, based on the biblical imperative as prescribed in Genesis 1. But this understanding has also come under criticism from some eco-theologians as it does not give to the earth its integrity, and by placing human beings "outside" creation it does not see all life – human and other – as a community. Sallie McFague critiques the concept of stewardship as being, "couched in the language of conserving resources for future generations – an implicit acknowledgment of its usefulness to human beings".[34]

Wesley Granberg-Michaelson, formerly director of the Church and Society department of the World Council of Churches, is another Christian environmentalist who is critical about the traditional understanding of the concept of stewardship. Robert Booth Fowler, commenting on Granberg-Michaelson's position, writes,

> The Bible stresses God's care for the earth and our duty to nurture creation as God's wish. Thus for him [Granberg-Michaelson], stewardship makes sense only in the metaphor of deep, complete caring. It has nothing to do with human authority in a hierarchical universe, including the authority to protect the rest of nature, since humanity is somehow both separated from it and superior to it. Granberg-Michaelson is equally impatient with much of the routine Christian endorsement of stewardship. As far as he is concerned it often amounts to little more than verbal pleasantries or Sunday morning pieties.[35]

The controversy surrounding the terms "stewardship" and "dominion" in ecumenical discussions was most visibly demonstrated at Canberra in 1991, at the seventh assembly of the World Council of Churches. Protestant representatives from the churches in Asia, Africa, the Pacific and Latin America pleaded for the use of the term "steward" – which they perceived as a distinction and high office of the human as steward or householder and tiller and keeper. Representatives from Europe and North America, however, "stood sober before 'dominion' and were fearful that 'steward' too, might easily slide into the imperial mastery they knew well".[36] Rasmussen recognizes that "from the perspective of the globally less powerful, to be named by God the custodians of creation and God's appointed, is an empowering word".[37] However, this does not make the anthropocentrism and homocentrism of the concept of stewardship less problematic and needs to be explored further.

The question asked by some theologians is why so much emphasis is placed on Genesis 1-2, on the sin-salvation motif and on the anthropocentrism of such texts alone. There is an unrecognized value in other parts of the Bible, which is more earth-loving. For example, Genesis chapters 4-11 with their communitarian focus; the dimension of social responsibility in Genesis chapter 4; and the sense of cosmic inter-relatedness (dramatized in the flood story and the universal covenant with all nations and all creation). Additionally, we have not looked holistically on the plurality of creation stories in the Bible evidenced in the Psalms, Deutero-Isaiah and the Wisdom books.[38]

Therefore, it is necessary to recover other biblical texts and make them more central to our discourse. Theology needs to find alternative ways to structure our relationships with God and with the earth and the need of the hour is to find the spiritual resources to do this. Additionally, some of the critique of Western patriarchal theology needs to address third-world liberation theology, too.

Third-world liberation theologies

When third-world liberation theologies emerged some thirty years ago, they were without a doubt a watershed in theology. Theologians from Latin America, Asia and Africa, as well as minorities in North America through movements such as the EATWOT (the Ecumenical Association of Third World Theologians), have contributed important and alternative ways of doing theology. They have broken away from what is not helpful in inherited theologies so as to courageously interpret the Bible and Christian doctrines from the perspective of the struggles for liberation of peoples, each theologian from his or her own context. This affirmation of the social location of the reader of the Bible as opposed to universal and homogenous interpretations, as traditional theologies tend to demand, has been a source of hope for many people. Liberation theologies offered spiritual resources for political actions for transformation of unjust structures and institutions. Additionally it opened the way for interpretations of Christian scriptures in the midst of diverse cultures and in dialogue with many religious contexts in which theological activity takes place in the third world.

Yet, from the perspective of the integrity of the earth, liberation theologies too can be faulted for being essentially anthropocentric and human centred in their approach because solidarity with the poor and marginalized humanity is the key of these theologies. George Matthew Nalunnakkal, an Indian eco-theologian, believes that the reason for this anthropocentrism is the over-dependence on "the Marxist tools of social analysis" as the basis for much of third-world theological methodology.[39] Nalunnakkal hastens to affirm the contributions of liberation theologies and of Marx for the transformation of societies and injustice in our world, yet he laments that third-world theologians have, by and large, failed to appropriate their responsibility to respond to the ecological crisis. Nalunnakkal mentions a few liberation theologians that have begun looking at the liberation of creation as an integral part of the liberation story, but they remain isolated examples and they too have not made this commitment an integral part of their theology. Some have begun recognizing creation as "the new poor". He names Gustavo Gutiérrez, Leonardo Boff and K.C. Abraham who in their more recent writings have attempted to "transcend the Marxist analysis of society" so as to make their theologies "relevant for tomorrow". This has been rooted in their attempts "to treat ecological problems as part of the socio-economic problems of the poor".[40] But most third-world male theologians have a long way to go.

Interestingly, Nalunnakkal has not included the writings of third-world women theologians in this frame of critique. He does review the work of a few third-world women in his chapter on eco-feminist theology, but in the chapter on liberation theologies he leaves out the extensive contributions of women liberation theologians. Ivone Gebara as well as Chung Hyun Kyung, Kwok Pui Lan and my own writings could, for example, be read as a critique of the limitations of traditional third-world male theologians and liberation theologians in addressing eco-theological concerns. All of us women theologians have found our roots in liberation theology but have asked for a more holistic approach.

Third-world women theologians agree with their male counterparts that the plight of the poor is of critical importance, as is the development of a spirituality centred on the struggles of the poor for liberation from various forms of oppression. However, they urge an equal emphasis on the struggles of the earth for its integrity. Ivone Gebara, as an example, classifies all oppression as "social sin". But then to her the problem is that

> the fundamentally anthropocentric and androcentric character of liberation theology appears unquestionable. It speaks of God in human history, a God who in the end remains the Creator and Lord. It thereby reaffirms the entire Thomistic tradition on God and on the incarnation. It senses no need to re-examine the cosmological and anthropological foundations of Christian faith. It reaffirms the goodness and justice of God's being without raising questions about the repercussions, throughout human history, of traditional or historically conditioned images of God.[41]

This being the case, it is important to analyze why third-world theology has been so anthropocentric in its methodology and focus. To illustrate this, I share an experience.

"Please do not ask us to be less anthropocentric, when it is only now that we Dalits are 'becoming a people' who can speak of our lives and dignity as human beings." These words of a Dalit student, presently working on a doctoral thesis under the guidance of Chung Hyun Kyung at Union Theological Seminary in New York, have haunted me ever since I heard them.[42] What else can this Dalit woman have been expected to say? She says this because she represents the "Dalits" – a community newly learning to resist centuries of ritual and economic violence and exclusion. The Dalit woman represents communities in India that have lived in closest proximity to the earth and have nurtured the earth and its resources through prudent care. And yet it is only now, in the last few decades, because of the organized efforts of Dalits for dignity and justice, that they are emerging as a people. However, it is also true that poverty and deprivation have led to the erosion of many of their practices of prudent care of the earth and its resources.

Such realities challenge us as a faith community to sharpen the definition of anthropocentrism within a historical/anthropological framework. While the integrity of the earth needs to be safeguarded, aggressive anthropocentrism too needs to be challenged at all times. Our understanding of "anthropocentrism" therefore has to be corrected by recognition of the history of injustice experienced by some sections of our communities – because of their race, their caste or their ethnic origins. Speaking of the integrity of creation from the context of the earth community is a way out – this will be discussed later.

I maintain that liberation theology has this yet within its resources to offer to eco-theology because of its potential to provide the paradigm shift we so urgently need.

Indigenous peoples both within the third-world theological movement and in the ecumenical movement have always taken a more creation-centred approach and can be said to have impacted the WCC's work, even if only marginally. For example, they have been explicit in their critique of the concept of "stewardship". Rasmussen records the discussion at the Canberra assembly of the WCC in 1991 and the discontent of the Indigenous peoples represented there with the use of the term.

> These [Indigenous] peoples knew stewardship as the flipside of its message of empowerment for subjugated peoples. They knew stewardship as the ideology of the "civilizers" who had promulgated neo-European ways laced with imperialistic and racist notions. This was stewardship as spoken of by those "subduing the earth", but as now remembered by the subdued.[43]

On one issue there is near consensus in the ecumenical movement – that "the earth is the Lord's".[44] However, even on this count Indigenous peoples have expressed their concerns. At the WCC world convocation on Justice, Peace and the Integrity of Creation held in Seoul, Korea, in 1990, one of the ten affirmations made stated that "the earth is the Lord's". Tink Tinker, Lutheran theologian from the Osage peoples, reflecting on this later said that this is not acceptable to Indigenous peoples because it places God outside of creation – it makes God the "Lord", the "owner" of creation and this denies to the earth its integrity.[45] To Indigenous peoples, "the entire cosmos is the sacred community, and life should be lived with the respect and treatment due to the sacred – it's that simple and profound".[46] Rasmussen reminds us, "It means that all life, not just human life, shares a common moral universe... Aboriginal traditions have assumed this. Most modern ones have not."[47] The primal vision of eco-system peoples is essentially sacramental.

Orthodox contributions to ecumenical eco-theology

Sacramental theology has also been the cornerstone of Orthodox contributions to ecumenical eco-theology. Orthodox communities have, since the early centuries, understood the "sacraments as dramatizations of nature's transfiguration. Humans' high calling is as 'priests of creation', referring the creation back to the Creator in acts of liturgical doxology."[48] In other words, to the Orthodox, human beings are given a role for the "divinization" of nature, placing humanity in inter-relationship with creation and God. Georgian Orthodox woman theologian Tamara Grdzelidze writes,

> The church blesses the waters at the feast of the Epiphany and blesses the fruits at the feast of the Transfiguration as a sign of the recognition of the transformation of all creation through salvation and glorification. By the blessing of material things we are reminded that God's creation is sanctified, and that each part of this creation is of utmost importance: nature is sanctified, the world is a dwelling place of divine powers. Here we face the paradox of the Triune God being at the same time transcendent *and* immanent to his creation.[49]

Sacramentalism celebrates the divine in and with all nature – this includes human beings. In the creation psalms, thanks are offered for the sun, for the light, for the heavens and for fertility. The human being is thanking God, not merely on behalf of human beings but also in the name of heaven and earth and all created beings in them. This is not meant anthropomorphically or homocentrically. Creation cannot speak for itself; human beings are simply the tellers of its tale in a central way.[50]

Therefore, the Orthodox church believes that the solution to the ecological crisis lies in the liturgical, eucharistic and ascetic ethos of the Orthodox tradition and not in a renovation of ethics. This way of interpreting one's faith belongs largely to the Protestant tradition. An inter-Orthodox conference on environmental protection held in Crete in November 1991 set the agenda for the church. It was stated, "The Orthodox church shares the sensitivity and the concern of those who are distressed about the increasing burden on the natural environment due to human abuse, which the church names as *sin*, and for which it calls all human beings to *repentance*."[51]

Gennadios Limouris, Orthodox theologian, takes a slightly different view. He believes that it is in the creation context that ethics and ecclesiology are grounded. Therefore, some societal questions and problems will occasionally find their solutions within the ecclesial reality of the church. It is for this reason that the church is challenged to confront the living issue of justice and peace and the integrity of creation in radically new ways and according to radically new patterns of *koinonia*.[52]

The Orthodox contribution has concentrated on seeing the human being as the "microcosm" of the whole creation, stressing on the inextricable link between God, humanity and the rest of creation. The emphasis is on the human's freedom to be co-worker with God, or for the priestly function for a reintegrated and reconfigured creation. Creation doctrine as presented by Orthodox theologians is presented along traditional lines of creation *ex nihilo,* and there is an insistence that the cosmos has integrity of its own and reflects the beauty of the Creator.[53] Commenting on the Orthodox contributions to the debate, Geraldine Smyth writes,

> The word "wholeness" recurs. But there is suggestion of a dualism between humanity and the non-human creation in the reference to the Cappodocian image of the earth pictured as a beautiful palace into which God leads humanity. The perspective too is largely anthropocentric in the sense that creation is presented as deriving its value not only from its intrinsic goodness but from its appointment from God to be the home for living beings.[54]

The trinitarian view of creation is the other major contribution of the Orthodox churches. It is consistent with the understanding that God is essentially and not just economically relational. Feminist theologians such as Ivone Gebara, C.M. LaCugna, Hyun Kyung Chung, Mercy Amba Oduyoye and also male liberation theologians such as Leonardo Boff have also emphasized such a view. The trinitarian view with its relational understanding of God is an appropriate model to be explored for a new eco-theology.

For example, Gebara speaks of the need to translate anew the Trinity, which she describes as a "code that needs to be broken" out of its present limited interpretation. She offers the image of the earth as Trinity. "The trinitarian earth is a movement of continuous creativity, unfolding processes of creation and destruction, expressions of a single vital process."[55] Gebara calls this shift in understanding of God and the Trinity as "a spiritual path" we must take in nurturing the earth. She writes, "It is a spiritual path because it is the path of the Spirit, which blows freely where it wills; no one can hold back its movement. It is a spiritual path because it is the path of God in each and all of us."[56]

The integrity of creation

This takes us to the ecumenical movement's contributions to the notion of "the integrity of creation" and the World Council of Churches' processes that have affirmed this approach to the earth. As early as the second assembly of the WCC in Evanston in 1954, the essential goodness of creation was affirmed: "This world disfigured and distorted as it is, is still God's world. It is his creation, in which He is at work, and which He sustains in being until the day when the glory of his new creation will fully appear."[57] Yet, in the early years and because of the context in which the WCC was being formed, the focus concentrated on the well-being of the human creature and little was written from the perspective of the rest of creation. This was because the member churches at that time were preoccupied with the wounds of the world wars. To some churches the focus was on colonialism and the poverty it had generated in many parts of the world. Additionally, several nations were engaged in struggles for political freedom and independence. Therefore, the concerns of the WCC, at that time, were perhaps inevitably anthropocentric and androcentric too.

This language dominated the discourse till 1983 when the WCC met for its sixth assembly in Vancouver. Here the presence and participation of Native Canadian and other Indigenous peoples joined voices with environmentalists and some theologians who emphasized the devastation being done to the earth. By their gentle presence the Indigenous peoples reminded the assembly that the land on which the assembly was taking place (the University of British Columbia) was in fact sacred land that had originally belonged to the Indigenous peoples of the country. They brought to the consciousness of the assembly their creation-centred spirituality. The theme Justice, Peace and the Integrity of Creation (JPIC) was announced both as a commitment as well as a programme direction for the churches through the WCC. The assembly called the churches to a conciliar process of mutual commitment and covenanting on the inter-related concerns for justice, for peace and for the integrity of creation. The decision was taken shortly thereafter at a central committee of the WCC to call for a world convocation on Justice, Peace and the Integrity of Creation to be held in Seoul, Korea, in 1989.

In preparation for the world convocation, a consultation in Granvollen, Norway, in 1988 brought together some forty theologians, church leaders, women and Indigenous peoples to unravel further the phrase "integrity of creation" embedded in JPIC. The final statement in Granvollen acknowledged the wisdom and contributions of women, blacks and Indigenous peoples in caring for the earth.[58] But it also said more. It affirmed that creation "possesses an inner cohesion and goodness" by virtue of its origins in "the will and love of the triune God". Moreover, it announced that it is not humanity that "integrates" creation. Creation's integrity "is prior to our concern, prior to our participation".[59] The consultation marked an epistemological break in ecumenical creation theology with the often-muted voices of women and other groups on the periphery becoming stronger. The Granvollen statement asserted,

> The drive to have "mastery" over creation has resulted in the senseless exploitation of natural resources, the alienation of the land from people and the destruction of Indigenous cultures. It ignores the experience of oppressed peoples like the blacks and women who suffer under its weight. It also undermines other highly developed systems of scientific, religious and philosophical thought. For example, Western medicine as it developed and spread over the world began to supplant Indigenous systems of medicine, which have a more holistic approach to health care and healing.[60]

It also stated,

> Creation came into being by the will and love of the triune God, and as such it possesses an inner cohesion and goodness. Though human eyes may not always discern it, every creature and the whole creation in chorus bear witness to the glorious unity and harmony with which the creation is endowed.[61]

This was an "epistemological break" because for the first time the WCC process seemed to heed the voice of the earth and of eco-system peoples. The statement from Granvollen therefore demonstrates "the church's readiness to consider the creation for its own sake and not only in the setting of the human drama".[62] Granvollen showed that women and Indigenous peoples have a vested interest in caring for the earth because of their own victimization and vulnerability, but also because of their "yearning and gift for healing, and their sense of God as dynamic and inter-relational with creation".[63] Geraldine Smyth acknowledges that after Granvollen, Indigenous theology

> calling for pre-eminence for creation, for the sake of creation, is posing an urgent challenge to the theological enterprise... The yearning for the wholeness and totality of creation among Indigenous peoples finds its gospel correlative in the vision of the kingdom conceived not primarily in temporal but in spatial terms. Because God reigns in this space, it is a metaphor for the whole of creation.[64]

At the world convocation on JPIC in Seoul, the earth was at the centre of the reflections. This is underlined by Larry Rasmussen, who describes beautifully the closing worship in Seoul:

> A replica of planet earth was part of the closing worship... Borne to the centre of the assembly by children of different colours, languages, and cultures, the earth was the object of the children's message to the delegates: "Treat earth gingerly; pray and plead for its future; pray and plead for ours." Then the entire assembly, representing most of historic Christianity and every race and region was invited to come forward and lay hands quietly on the earth. They came and touched, in gratitude

> and blessing... Given two millennia of Christian ambivalence about earth loyalties and strong taboos about pagan nature religions, did those delegates fully understand the significance of placing earth at the centre? Did they comprehend the ritual they performed with such sincerity and the commitments they prayed with such earnestness?[65]

The questions he raises remain, in spite of the work done so far. It is an unfinished agenda. It also has to be acknowledged that Seoul was far from smooth. There was criticism from those engaged in struggles for social justice, particularly from the Southern hemisphere that the rising priority on environmental concerns was a "Northern and largely middle-class diversion of the churches attention from the more critical concerns of hunger, poverty and racial justice".[66] Holding together the commitment to the earth and to social and economic justice remains a challenge.

In the present phase of its work, the WCC has participated in and monitored the UN discussions on sustainable development as an entry point for its work on creation. An ecumenical delegation participated in the 1972 Earth Summit organized by the United Nations in Rio de Janeiro in Brazil. Rio set in place what is called the Agenda 21 of actions governments need to take to reverse some of the damage done to the earth. Rio gave the impetus for the conventions on climate change and bio-diversity as well as other international legal provisions to monitor the use of the resources of the earth. The Rio process, however, did not challenge the neo-liberal economic path that is at the heart of the problem and it did not question the earth threatening growth oriented development paradigm. In fact, Rio re-launched some of the "development-as-growth" policies.

The WCC has been involved in "development" as a basic human right for over forty years now. However, development has always been viewed from the context of the development of communities. It has not accepted the dominant definition of development i.e. as economic growth.[67] Therefore, WCC popularized the expression "sustainable communities" and has refused the term "sustainable development" as it has been critiqued as a contradiction in terms. Sustainable development assumes the centrality of the market economy and then moves out towards ecological considerations.[68] In 1997, the WCC delegation to the fifth session of UNCED said,

> We find it [the concept sustainable development] often misused in order to legitimize current economic approaches which are premised on unlimited economic growth and a continuous and unregulated expansion of production and consumption for the world's rich. Thus to measure progress towards sustainable development in this context is to avoid challenging the very dynamics which are increasing the gap between the rich and the poor in the world and causing environmental destruction. We call on governments, international institutions and people of goodwill to demonstrate moral courage and political will to confront the excesses of globalization.[69]

Sustainable development and sustainable communities are on different paths. As Larry Rasmussen's describes it,

> Sustainable development is not the preferred direction. Sustainable community is. Sustainable development and sustainable community are contrasting paths into the future. They carry different notions of the structure of human society and responsibility. The differences turn most of all on the issues that most impact nature and earth as communities: namely, the globalizing economy and the distribution of power among the peoples of the world.[70]

However, this has not stopped the WCC from participating in a variety of world events where this term has been "liberally employed" such as the UNCED gathering in Rio and the Third Conference of Parties in Kyoto, and the meetings of the Commission on Sustainable Development.[71] But the WCC's participation has always been tinged with a language of critique. This includes the meeting of the World Summit on Sustainable Development in Johannesburg in August-September 2002, and the more recent meeting of the WSSD in New York in 2005, referred to earlier. In Johannesburg, one of the focus points of the ecumenical presence was to challenge the corruption of power and the way it is wielded by governments in close connection with business interests. The delegation called for a legally binding international agreement on corporate accountability. The question of the abuse of corporate power has long been on the agenda of the ecumenical community. In preparation for the World Social Development Summit in Johannesburg, one of the WCC "talking points" states,

> Accountability is key to building trust and realization of human dignity and development within secure and sustainable communities. Such communities require a just and moral economy where people are empowered to participate in decisions affecting their lives, where the power is balanced and shared among government, business and civil society; and where public and private institutions are held accountable for the social and environmental consequences of their operations.[72]

Among the other concerns of the ecumenical team to Johannesburg was included the call to national governments to assert their responsibility regarding corporate licence to operate and create or strengthen government mechanisms and institutions as well as civil society organizations that promote accountability and support access to justice. At the international level the call was to the UN to reinstitute the Commission on Transnational Corporations to establish regulatory mechanisms for the relationship between corporate policies and practices and international obligations. The need was expressed to accelerate the drafting of universal human rights guidelines for companies to monitor their own activities. Additionally, the ecumenical call was for a legally binding framework convention for corporate accountability under the UN system which would include mandatory compliance with principles of corporate responsibility and enforceable codes of conduct, operational transparency, financial and legal liability for companies and company directors, as well as sanctions. Finally, it would require full and meaningful stakeholder participation and respect for Indigenous people's rights.[73]

The fact that we have a long way to go is evident from the growing power of institutions such as the World Economic Forum (WEF), a non-profit Geneva-based foundation which is described as being "dedicated to entrepreneurship in the global public interest". Every year the WEF brings together at Davos, Switzerland, governments and business in partnership. Klaus Schwab, president and founder of the WEF, claims that it is wrong to expect corporations to take on social responsibility. In his words,

> The role of business has become confusing. In this era of slow economic growth, we must re-embrace the wealth-enhancing, job-creating role that business plays in society. And business leaders must once again take the lead, offering up an assertive, positive vision of their function in the world at large... Like many people, we at the WEF welcome some elements of the corporate responsibility movement… But I worry, sometimes, that the trend towards saddling companies with social responsibilities may have gone too far. After all, economic growth is the business of business. If economies do not grow, there won't be enough wealth to meet the world's pressing needs, like finding a cure for AIDS or preserving the environment.[74]

While it was the JPIC process that began the process of holding together justice and creation as interlocked concerns, it is only in more recent years that specific efforts have been made to analyze globalization's deleterious impact not only on the poor but on the survival rights of creation as well. As Martin Robra, who heads the work on the environment in the WCC, describes this,

> The threats to the whole community of life – the global inequalities; climate change; loss of species and bio-diversity as well as topsoil, safe water, the wetlands; resource depletion and numerous wars – require that we address the social and ecological dimensions together in a humanly dominated biosphere. This is the major reason why the WCC's programmes on economic justice and ecology are becoming one common programme on economic globalization.[75]

In preparation for the World Summit on Sustainable Development in Johannesburg in 2002, the WCC organized a conference on ecology and faith under the title "Land, Water and Air: People Struggling for Life in a Globalizing Economy", in Bangalore, India, in December 2001. Here land, water and air were seen as vital resources and yet are all heavily polluted. The privatization of water, the alienation of peoples (particularly Indigenous peoples) from the land due to mining, the erosion of forests, the privatization of land for corporate expansion and the pollution of the air by industrialization (e.g. the Union Carbide factory's gas leak in Bhopal, India) – all are emblematic of the injustice in a global economy. Additionally, the conference was concerned that, "Globalization goes beyond direct attack on land to monopolization of Indigenous knowledge systems, which are sustainable and eco-friendly by their very nature. TRIPS and other international conventions thus legalize bio-piracy in favour of bio-technology."[76]

The ethics of food security, the peddling of GMO foods (genetically modified organisms), and the genetic manipulation of life forms are now coming on to the agenda of the WCC in a big way. Work on this has just begun. It calls on the churches to engage in issues that normally do not come within their range of commitment. As women, our feminist responses need to embrace the breadth of issues the WCC addresses in its political engagement for eco-justice.

Therefore the women's programme of the WCC has contributed to the WCC's work on economic globalization by providing a space for women's experiences and perspectives on economy to influence this work. It has attempted to harvest women's creative and practical survival strategies as alternatives to globalization. It has built a global network of feminist economists and women's groups from the churches who in a meeting in Geneva in February 2003 developed the concept of *a caring economy.* They said that a caring economy is rooted in justice and equity, but goes beyond that to recognize the value of social reproduction and not just economic production. Efficiency of this economy is considered in light of social costs and benefits. Caring and care work are made visible, (re)valued, (re)affirmed, (re)produced and (re)distributed equitably by both women and men. Additionally, a caring economy is seen in the light of *oikonomia*, as a wider and broader way of organizing life as a whole. It is about communities experiencing life together, of relationships, mutuality and reciprocity and not about individual satisfaction and competition. Participation of all in defining, planning and making a caring economy work is crucial. Human rights of all – including the economic, social and cultural rights of women – are protected. A caring economy moves away from values of accumulation and profit to values of redistribution and reparation. Plurality and contextuality are celebrated over universality and power is not linked to markets or free trade. Just and responsible trade and care for the earth are its hallmarks.[77] It is about the transformation of injustice in our world – and is not just about reformation.

Transformation or reformation? The ecumenical dialogue explored

There is fortunately unanimity of opinion in the ecumenical movement that something is seriously wrong with the state of our earth today. The churches together have affirmed:

> We will resist the claim that anything in creation is merely a resource for human exploitation. We will resist species extinction for human benefit; consumerism and harmful mass production; pollution of land, air and water; all human activities which are now leading to probable rapid climate change; and policies and plans which contribute to the disintegration of creation.[78]

There is unanimity in the understanding that the neo-liberal form of globalization has exposed three deleterious impacts on the earth. First, that the professed goal of globalization is to expand and therefore economic growth is spreading. But the outflow of capital from the "developed" world goes hand in hand with a historically outdated model of development. Second, that this has turned all commons into commodities and has led to the so-called "developing" part of the world throwing to the wind any form of sustainability so as to accelerate the exploitation of natural resources. (For example, Russia sold the treasures of Siberia, Senegal offered fishing rights to Spain and Japan, Mexico facilitated forest exploitation after the peso crisis, as did Brazil and Indonesia. "In desperate times, governments have to sell even their 'family silverware'"!) And third, that governments often have to sacrifice their responsibility to protect public goods for the sake of private commercial players. Governments, in the present world, are unable to provide protection to their peoples against the negative impacts of globalization.[79] That all this is unacceptable and leads to a spiralling increase of poverty and injustice is not a contested fact. There is agreement among the churches that we cannot sustain this system much longer.

There is disagreement on how these challenges need to be addressed. There are two clear positions within the ecumenical movement, often in conflict with each other. Both claim their response to be in obedience to the ecumenical calling to help reverse some of the damage done to the earth.

This is expressed sometimes in the challenges of dealing with the differences between some who are determined to engage in international advocacy and the anxiety among some others as to whether the institutions of international governance are able to really hold governments to accountability. This is vitiated by the fact that WCC member churches are divided by their different ecclesiologies and different understandings of social ethics, which influences the way the churches can act and speak in communion. Regretfully, the place and interests of the particular church in a particular national context over-rides its commitment to take common ecumenical positions. The churches sometimes find themselves influenced by the expediency of the moment and are unable to transcend their individual loyalties. This leads to their neglecting the gospel imperative to defend life and to eradicate all that obstructs abundant life for all.

One group would assert that there is an alternative to the present world order. I will call them the "transformative group". Feminists within this group would fit the typology of "socialist eco-feminists". The transformative group would speak of alternatives to globalization, to the neo-liberal or "free-market" paradigm – that it is possible for a movement of transformation "towards a world more hospitable to people and mindful of nature is possible – and indeed indispensable".[80] Therefore, "Another World is Possible" is the slogan that has accompanied this group of the ecumenical movement that participates in the World Social Forum.[81] This has now become a yearly event and a rallying point for social movements who believe that an alternative world is not just desirable, it is possible. Drawing on the knowledge of eco-system peoples, the poor and excluded, this group would call for a restructuring of the world order to make it more caring of the earth and of its peoples. They would challenge the neo-liberal market project and the outdated and inappropriate development paradigm that accompanies it. They critique the neo-liberal economic framework that has taken the power of states and has placed it in the hands of the corporate sector and multinational enterprises.

On the other hand, there are those whom I call the "reformist groups". Feminists within this group would fit the typology of being "liberal eco-feminists". They would assume that there is no going back – that globalization is here to stay and therefore needs to be tamed and made environment-friendly. They would define the ecumenical task as staying in dialogue with those who wield power and to try to reform systems of injustice from within so as to reduce their impact on the poor and on the earth. It is this group which would focus attention on calling for conventions and legal provisions to protect the earth and its resources. Fair trade and other short-term answers through single-issue campaigns become the agenda of this group. There can be criticism that this group tends to focus more on the agenda set by global actors than by the people most affected by environmental degradation.

These two strands of political methodology have sometimes been in tension with each other. This is inevitable, given the complexity of the ecumenical movement. Martin Robra analyzes this tension and writes that it is the social locations and contextual conditions of different churches that lead to these diverse positions and perceptions of the consequences of economic globalization. Different frameworks of analysis and ethical discernment are formed by the different histories and relationships between individual churches, their societies and states.

> Representatives of churches from the South for example, often refer to the continuity of history of five hundred years of colonial oppression in the present global distribution and use of economic, political, cultural and military power that result in growing inequality and exclusion. Representatives from the Western European context tend to emphasis discontinuity, pointing to the end of the bipolar world system.

This leads to their favouring solutions for the new economic reality that are "modelled on institutional frameworks of the social compromise that marked their own societies during the cold-war period". Western European churches have their strong critique of the injustices as well as inequities within the present economic system but "do not see realistic alternatives to the work for changes within the system, although they recognize the 'democracy deficit' and inadequacy of existing global institutions". Churches from the South pressed by the urgency of the poverty around them and the struggles they see their communities experience, "call for tangible changes and visible support in response to God's call for justice as a real expression of the common calling as Christians in this world. They see the very being of the churches at stake in matters of injustice and the destruction of God's creation."[82]

But our faith demands that at all times the survival of the earth and the poor needs to stay as the focus of our attention. There are challenges ahead of us to green our faith, but

> the issue at the end is not whether rooted and realistic changes *can* be made, radical changes among them. They can. The issue rather is whether we can understand the place of faith and the ascendancy of ethics. Do we realize that the key to sustainability of inclusive nature rests in the character of the social order that is ours? Has it hit us full force that sustainability is less a matter of our wits than our collective moralities and cosmologies that it turns on justice, peace and the integrity of creation?[83]

The question is whether the churches are ready to make radical changes. It calls to question the place of the church within the framework of the political, economic and social power structures in their societies. It does question the responses of the churches to the neo-liberal economic paradigm and their tendency to take the route that is politically feasible rather than that which involves risk and a change of life-styles. All this in my estimation has ecclesiological implications and challenges the very being of the church – this is why it is difficult to address. Some ways out of this dilemma have been addressed in the work done by the WCC thus far.

The theology of life process: introducing the concept of the ecumenical earth, earth ethics

In the 1990s the WCC initiated the "theology of life" process as a way forward out of these sometimes dichotomized world-views. This process attempted to create an ecumenical space for a dialogue of life of many local experiences to build up common processes for ethical discernment leading to practical steps for common action in solidarity. Theology of life was not seen as a new theology. It simply responds to the challenge of the urgency to develop an alternative way of theologizing that places the poor and creation at the centre, with the goal being transformation.

Some of its premises:

- Theology of life de-centres Christianity and re-reads the Bible, theology, ecclesiologies and church practices.

- Theology of life entails a vision of ecumenical earth *(oikos)* an alternative to the project of globalization. The goal is the up building of just and sustainable communities *(oikodome)*.
- Theology of life is attentive to the life-giving practices in the different communities. It emerges from the social and religious practices of communities and aims at deeper community. It is deeply rooted in a spirituality growing from the life of people.[84]

The theology of life process did play an influencing role in holding together justice and the integrity of creation. Therefore, the eighth assembly of the WCC in Harare, Zimbabwe, in 1998, in its policy document on globalization, called for "a fundamental reshaping of the economic system" (this is far from a reformist position!). As the text put it,

> Sustainable development, a concept prominent in international flora, still leaves powerful forces of globalization in command and does not question the underlying paradigm of continuous and unlimited progress and growth. Affirming God's gift of life to all creation in the midst of pain, suffering and destruction caused by economic globalization, it is imperative to discern a life-centred vision.[85]

Here some of the traditional theological and biblical positions on creation were put to test. The assembly affirmed that

God's salvation in Jesus Christ not only means fullness of life for the human community, but the restoration of all creation to its goodness and wholeness. God's Holy Spirit comes to renew the whole creation. According to the creation stories of the Bible, the earth was meant to be home to all living creatures, which live in different spaces, but linked to each other in a web of relationships. The human community is placed within the wider community of the earth, which is embedded in God's household of life.[86]

The concepts of "ecumenical earth", and of "earth community" as the theological vision behind this, were restated. Sustainable communities and ecology were seen as one integrated whole defined as eco-justice. The assembly reaffirmed the WCC's commitment to stand in solidarity with those engaged in political movements for transforming unjust structures by calling for the upbuilding of just and sustainable communities, revitalizing and protecting the communities of Indigenous peoples, who engage in resistance against the growing domination of economic globalization. The statement described the four essentials for a life-centred vision: (1) participation of all; (2) equity as basic fairness that also extends to other life forms; (3) accountability as the structuring of responsibility towards one another and the earth itself; and (4) sufficiency as the commitment to meet basic needs of all but by developing the quality of life. This includes bread for all, but is more than bread alone.

By affirming creation's integrity we assert the Christian commitment to the earth and its distress, particularly in respecting the traditional wisdom of prudent care of those most affected by the destruction of the earth. We have seen the deep ecology that lies in traditions of prudence – those who have thus far been only peripheral in ecumenical discussions.

Drawing on the discussions of James Nash, Larry Rasmussen, who was key to the WCC's theology of life process, lists the biotic rights of all of creation to participate in the natural dynamics of existence without human interference and genetic alteration – to healthy and whole habitats; to reproduce their own kind without humanly-induced chemical or bio-engineered aberrations; to fulfil their evolutionary potential with freedom from human-induced extinctions; to freedom from human cruelty, or profligate use; to reparations or restitution to restore a semblance of natural conditions disrupted by human abuse; and the right to a "fair share" of goods necessary for individuals and species.[87] This earth ethic falls within the frame of the earth community, *oikos* (household) or the ecumenical earth as Rasmussen describes it – of humankind and other-kind as one whole. The work of the World Council of Churches on the environment has been designed around a commitment to the concepts of an earth ethic and the ecumenical earth.

As mentioned already the work on ecology is placed in close connection with the discussions on finding alternatives to economic globalization. Therefore, the natural corollary to the work on the cancellation of third-world economic debt has been the commitment to raise the issue of ecological debt – the users paying for the havoc they have caused in the world by the over-use of resources in past colonial history and in the present. Additionally, the concern is with environmental racism which intertwines the lives of oppressed human beings and polluted nature.

On the question of environmental racism, the WCC has initiated important discussions. It is built on the assumption that the dominant development paradigm has broken down community bonds and has psychic and cultural consequences, with the depletion of community-directed and prudently managed material resources. Therefore, participants in the WCC environmental justice movement would rather work for change in "the quality of life" rather than simply for a "cleaner natural environment".[88] Rasmussen speaks of "a three-dimensional nexus of economic injustice, social injustice and an unjust incidence of environmental quality, all of which overwhelmingly assures the continued oppression of communities of colour and low-income communities on environmental matters".[89]

The WCC study guide on overcoming racism includes a section on environmental racism. It acknowledges that Indigenous peoples as well as Africans and people of African descent see humanity as one with creation – of the human community and the wider earth community, belonging to each other. The study guide goes on to critique the prevailing economic and development paradigm and economic globalization that have ensured "racist patterns in the distribution of negative economic and environmental consequences". The African concept of *ubuntu* is lifted up as a cosmo-vision that embraces cultures, identities and traditions, customs and values that emphasize this inter-relatedness of life and creation.[90]

The eco-feminist ethic too has emphasized mutual interdependency that replaces hierarchies of domination, such as race. As Rosemary Radford Ruether describes this, "All racist, sexist, classist, cultural and anthropomorphic assumptions of the superiority of whites over blacks, males or females, managers over workers, humans over animals and plants, must be discarded."[91]

Therefore, the commitment to overcome environmental racism is accompanied by a challenge to all systems of domination that privilege some over others on the basis of race or ethnicity. The WCC challenges the racism embedded in both the expropriation of the land and livelihood of eco-system peoples as well as the expropriation of their knowledge systems.

This has been done in conjunction with overcoming sexism – recognizing the inter-relatedness of these concerns. For example, during the Ecumenical Decade of the Churches in Solidarity with Women (1988-98), an important network was initiated by the WCC called SISTERS – Sisters in Struggle to Eliminate Racism and Sexism. Among the issues identified for special attention during this Decade were the issues of economic injustice and the commitment to overcome racism because it was recognized that women, along with children, face the most deleterious impacts of globalization, of racism and the concurrent destruction of the earth.

Therefore, the challenge of environmental racism and sexism is not just an add-on to the programme but is an integral part of it. It is women's bodies and their livelihoods that are most wounded by scarcity in basic common goods such as forests, clean water and air. Therefore, the "debt to women" is an integral challenge in the globalization debate.

Feminist theologians agree that deep systemic changes are needed to develop a new ecological vision. As women we see the liberation of the poor and the well-being of nature as two sides of the same coin. The way in which the dominant economic model has imposed itself on the world and our inability to develop alternatives has been an issue of deep concern. An eco-feminist theological vision has much to offer to the ecumenical movement. This was the challenge reinforced by a small group of eco-feminist theologians who were invited to Geneva in July 2003 for a brainstorming session to reflect on the next steps of WCC's theological work on creation.[92]

The writings of eco-feminist theologians in all parts of the world formed the inspiration for the meeting. From the outset it was underlined that Christian theology has to change to become more earth-loving. The group affirmed the promise of alternative communities who live in a caring relationship to the earth and in opposition to corporate globalization. It was also acknowledged that alternative cosmologies and epistemologies of Indigenous peoples and other subordinated groups need to influence ecumenical theology. It was suggested that "case-studies" of selected alternative projects be visited and studied within a feminist analytical framework. This should lead to the development of an alternative theological vision and a recovery of the eco-dimensions of the Bible – that should be reread with new eco-feminist hermeneutic lenses.

Some of the issues identified by the women theologians for further reflection include: God's preferential option for the poor/for the earth; earth, body and matter; reclaiming the mystery, the sacred and the transcendent; sickness, alienation, suffering and death; justice, wellness and healing; community and celebration; and creativity, energy and new visions. Additionally, they asked: What is the historical role of Christianity in promoting colonialism and corporate globalization? Is there really an epistemological break or are we listening to the people who live in close proximity to the earth for the first time, and are we challenging the hegemony of Christianity? Can feminist analysis play a role in naming the empire and exposing the way the power to dominate plays out in our world? There was also a word of caution that there could be a new anthropocentrism in the earth community language –that needs to be challenged by a feminist and earth loving approach.

In a written reflection Rosemary Radford Ruether, who was one of the participants at this meeting, recognized that the WCC's work on Justice, Peace and Creation intentionally integrates these interdependent concerns. It also gave to nature its integrity, "as a subject in its own right, and not merely an object of human control and ownership". She emphasized that the process should move towards "networking in the churches to deal with the 'disintegration of the earth' and to propose practical grassroots alternatives and biblical/theological perspectives that support these alternatives".[93]

The ecumenical task is there before us – an eco-feminist theology that responds to the traditions of prudence of peoples subjugated to lower social ranks and to the political resistance movements of women. The song from Singhbhum accompanies us, "Let's knit it up, Let's plait it together again!"

4. Towards an Eco-feminist Theology

A long time ago,
when there was thick jungle here,
our ancestors were clearing the jungle
to make fields.
At that time, when they reached this spot,
the Spirit of this place, that we call Dessauli,
who lives in the Sal groves,
asked the people
not to cut down the Sal trees.

The Spirit told them,
"This is my home.
So let these trees remain.
I will be with you
and protect you from all evil.
In return you will make offerings to me
At Maghe Parab,
when you celebrate the harvest.
And at Ba-Parab,
When the Sal flower begins to bloom.
If you do this, I will protect you." [1]

A simple but deep faith that if the *Sal* trees are protected and if worship accompanies the seasons, then the people will be protected by Dessauli the divine Spirit that inhabits the forests! It is this deep spirituality that sustains the Indigenous Peoples of India and all over the world. Is there something Christianity can learn from such a spiritual interdependence with the earth so that it too can become more earth-centred? What from Christianity can the ecumenical movement reclaim to restore its potential to strengthen earth community and an earth ethic? Jay McDaniel cautions,

> Heretofore, most of the classical spiritual traditions, with the possible exception of Taoism, have not been particularly good at encouraging environmental awareness and sensitivity. As Thomas Berry has suggested, they have been better at human-human relations and human-divine relations than human-earth relations. By contrast the Indigenous spiritual traditions – the

> ways of Native American, Aborigines and Africans, for example – have been more earth-centred. Their way to God has been through the earth.[2]

He goes on to recognize that eco-system peoples have not always been ecologically benign, but then, it is not necessary to romanticize their treatments of the earth so as to recognize the value of their spiritual interconnections with the earth. Each Indigenous tribe through its rituals, festivals and spiritual beliefs sustains relationships to the land – yet we ignore their voices of sanity and reason. Traditions of prudent care by which eco-system peoples have survived for centuries, turn us to the earth and the wisdom of the earth, a turn that Christianity so urgently needs.

The theme of the ninth assembly of the World Council of Churches in Porto Alegre, Brazil, in February 2006 is "God, in Your Grace, Transform the World", which centres on the doctrine of grace. This could be a theological entry-point for this discussion. Can we make an ecological enquiry into the doctrine of grace? This theme challenges the church and Christians to engage in transformative justice in the world – justice that the world so desperately needs! It was later decided that one of the sub-themes of the assembly would be "God, in Your Grace, Transform the Earth". If we focus only on "transform the world" there is danger of excessive anthropocentrism. In the concepts of ecumenical earth and earth community, the term "earth" includes the world – it holds all of creation together in its embrace. The word "world", however, has traditionally been limited to human life. For example, commentaries on the John 3:16 text "God so loved the world" usually refer only to the world of human beings, of fallen humanity who will be redeemed by the Son.

The Greek word for the world, cosmos, refers to the sinful reality in which human beings live and this draws us to the image of the cosmic Christ. Exegetes speak of reconciled humanity or a new transformed human race as being the fruits of the saving grace of God. Tink Tinker, the Osage theologian, reflecting on the traditional (Euro-Christian) understanding of the cosmic Christ, writes,

> God's salvific act in Christ Jesus is thought of as efficacious only for human beings, and hence God's salvific love for the world must imply logically that the world is here limited only to those who are most privileged in creation and are the proper object of God's affections. The danger of such privileging of human beings should be obvious. It runs the risk of generating human arrogance, which too easily sees the world in terms of hierarchies of existence, all of which are ultimately subservient to the needs and whims of humans.[3]

There is real danger therefore that the Porto Alegre theme "God, in Your Grace, Transform the World" will continue with this stream of anthropocentrism. The theme does not immediately stir up the sense of awe and wonder about all of God's creation, nor does it easily evoke the urgently needed deep remorse for what we as human beings have done to the earth. Such a challenge was more evident in the theme of the seventh assembly of the WCC, held in Canberra in 1991 (over a decade ago!) "Come, Holy Spirit – Renew the Whole Creation". This was the last time a WCC assembly theme had expressed a direct commitment to the earth. Canberra's theme had inspired the theological space for strengthening the work WCC has done on creation. A theme of an Assembly does have the possibility of providing the backdrop for developing theological reflections and can impact future programmatic work and therefore the need to discover the ecological possibilities of the Porto Alegre theme, "God, in Your Grace, Transform the World".

Two key words "grace" and "God" offer a word of hope in this direction. By including the element of transformation the theme does respond well to the present phase of the work of holding economy and ecology together – of recognizing the integral link between the globalization project and political action to protect the earth. The theme also does offer us the possibility of turning to God as the source of grace and transformation. However, for the purposes of claiming the theme for its potential in offering resources for an earth ethic and theology in this book I shall now reflect on two aspects of it: first the doctrine of grace, and second the way God is imaged in the context of a broken creation. The traditional understandings of these two concepts need to be deconstructed so as to uncover their liberating possibilities, and then they need to be reconstructed through an eco-feminist lens.

The doctrine of grace

Grace is understood as God's mercy and power, God recovering individual persons from sin, while granting them new life.[4] Grace is seen as God's *free action* for the benefit of humanity. In fact it is considered "one of the central concepts of Christian theology, even considered at times to be the quintessence of Christianity as a whole."[5] In another definition, grace is fundamentally understood as "God's mercy and power, apart from humans, whereby God recovers individual persons from sin while granting forgiveness and new life".[6] In the Old Testament, the word *Q'en* in Hebrew is related to benevolence of a person with authority, most of the times a king towards a vassal (e.g. Esther 8:5 ff. where the Queen Esther claims from King Ahasuerus his grace). The word grace is often linked in the OT to two other Hebrew words *hesed* and *hemet* – mercy and faithfulness. Traditionally, it is understood that God's grace is given unconditionally. It is a dependable promise. One who asks in prayer to have it can have it. Grace is even given precedence over the commandment.[7]

However, some exegetes underline the fact that God's acts of "favour" in the wilderness establish a relationship of mutual obligations. An initial gift of "un-coerced favour" leads to the form of relationship in which the benefactor will continue to provide assistance, and the beneficiaries will remain "singularly loyal" to the benefactor and will need to offer services to the benefactor.[8] The promise of a covenant depicts a God of grace who demands our "co-creative" response. Traditional understandings of grace tend to view the relationship between God and humankind as "symmetrical and opposing", according to liberation theologian José Míguez Bonino. Most often it is the power of

God that is affirmed, diminishing the importance of human participation. Bonino believes that the promise of the covenant offered by the grace of God does not reduce God's "partner" (co-creator), even an unfaithful partner, to an object. Rather, the covenant directs itself to the human being, invites that being to respond, and to act, and in that way holds open permanently the door to human collaboration with God.[9]

In the New Testament, the equivalent for the term "grace" is the Greek term *charis*. Paul uses this word several times and the doctrine of grace is central to his theology. The epistle to the Romans is of importance here. Paul emphasizes the gracious action of God towards humanity in the death of Jesus Christ (Rom. 3-6), and the presence of God's grace in believers (Rom. 5:1-11, 6:14; 2 Cor. 6:1; Gal. 1:6; Phil.1:7). The fullness of the various charismata as gifts of God corresponds to the *charis* bestowed by God and makes that *charis* a reality in the Christian community (Rom. 12:3-21; 1 Cor.1:4-9). The incarnation is that act of God giving Godself so that humanity can know and love God. Romans 5:12-21 equates this eschatological divine act of grace in justification with the love of God revealed in Jesus' death for sinners. Grace annihilates the power of sin and death in the eternal life of those who are made perfect. Romans 6 describes how the baptized and justified have died with Christ to sin and are no longer under the law but are under grace (v.14) and therefore have the prospect of eternal life as a gift *(charisma)* of the freely given grace of God (v.23).

In the early church and the middle ages, grace was seen only in a soteriological and ethical context. The understanding was that salvation could be achieved through a conjunction of divine and human action. God's action establishes the comprehensive and definitive starting point of the human road to salvation and also provides for the final goal. But between start and finish lie human ethics and morals made possible by grace as a life in grace and also as the appropriation and demonstration of grace in moral behaviour and as indispensable for salvation.[10]

From the time of Irenaeus (late 2nd century), the church was identified as the place where grace is found. For Athanasius, Christ is the mediator of grace in creation and redemption. The connection of grace and the Spirit was important especially in Eastern theology, e.g. for Basil the Great. Gregory of Nyssa placed the connection between divine grace and the moral behaviour of human beings in relation to salvation as *synergia* (synergy) while John Chrysostom puts the main emphasis on grace. In Western theology Augustine set the course, influenced by Paul's theology, of switching from a Platonic theory of knowledge to an interest in how right action is made possible. He also understood sin anew: to him human beings are intrinsically characterized by sin, which is expressed in covetousness, greed and self-love. Only God can open up the self-centredness of humanity. Therefore it is only the grace of God that enables humanity not only to do good but even to will to do good. As with Paul, Augustine too believed that grace is freely given without the prior works of human beings. This placed Eastern and Western theology on conflicting paths. Gregory I challenged the position of Augustine and insisted that grace starts with the conversion of sinful human beings through faith and the will to do good, accompanies them at baptism and together with free will is the cause of good works. Therefore, human cooperation is indispensable for conversion and for good works. But Gregory I also stated that that there can be no Christian existence without grace.[11] To Thomas Aquinas, faith, hope and love follow from grace. To him, grace is the entrance of the eternal love of God into the human ego.

To the Reformation thinkers the theme of grace was central. Grace was an essential ingredient of Luther's doctrine of justification. He followed Augustine's theology by stressing that the gospel of Christ is grace. God accepts believers who look in faith on Christ and justifies sinners by grace alone without any merit on their part – since Christ has through his death overcome human sin. For Calvin, too, the divine sovereignty in God's gracious acts is decisive. This has largely been the position of Protestant theologians to this day.

This very brief and quick overview of biblical and traditional understandings of the doctrine of grace indicates that over the centuries this theme has been affirmed and often reinterpreted and nuanced and has figured in disputes over its own definition, particularly in the Protestant church. Therefore it offers itself for reinterpretation and reappropriation as a theme for today's ecological task. One dilemma here is that traditional understandings of the doctrine of grace in Protestant theology all tend to focus on an open-ended understanding of humanity and on human relationships with God.

Shifts in the theological understanding of grace

A shift in the way grace is understood came with liberation theologians who reclaimed the power of the doctrine of grace in the context of the struggles of the poor – they qualified the understanding of humanity by adding the dimension of God's option for the poor. Elsa Tamez, from Mexico/Costa Rica, as a third-world feminist theologian underlines that though all human beings "manifest a broken image of God (the victimizers as well as victims), God chooses a meeting place so that God's image might be reproduced in every living being". But she underlines that,

> God makes this choice not in order to exclude some people, but precisely in order to negate exclusion by including all people beginning with those presently excluded. God's preferential option is to begin with the excluded who cry out to God in their abandonment – who know they are excluded and who demand from the God of life the end of God's absence.[12]

Can we listen also to the wounded and excluded voice of the earth?

Leonardo Boff calls for a new interpretation of the theme of grace to respond to the present challenges. He acknowledges that "we already live in the *divine milieu* of grace" and "the problem for theology is how to deal with that fact thematically, how to speak about grace in a meaningful way today. We do not want an outdated idiom to keep people from taking cognizance of the full depth and meaning of something they are actually living. The fact is that human beings are living the experience of grace, but they may not know it or reflect on it."[13] To him, theologically "grace does not begin to exist when we talk about it. We talk about it because it first exists in our lives. We may experience real grace and the presence of God without ever using those terms." Therefore it always reflects the present reality, and therefore each community's present context. "Its aim is not to monopolize grace but to make human beings aware of the grace that is visiting their lives."[14]

However, even liberation theologians such as José Míguez Bonino, Leonardo Boff and Elsa Tamez tend to overemphasize an anthropocentric view. One way out is to draw inspiration from those liberation theologians, particularly Leonardo Boff and Ivone Gebara, who speak of "the earth as the new poor".[15] The emphasis should be on creation as the "excluded" by the dominant economic globalization project, and on how the earth and people will need to be liberated together so that both can thrive, or not at all.[16] Additionally, the rights attributed to the earth include the rights of *all* of humankind (not just some) to live and survive.

The way in which we have abused the earth can only be described in the words of Leonardo Boff as "*disgrace,* sin and perdition."[17] Grace, to Boff,

> is the absolute meaning that brings fulfilment to everything and makes all comprehensible. *Dis-grace* is absolute absurdity, sheer darkness without a trace of light. It has no rationale. There is no logical argument for dis-grace and sin, which cannot be understood in any way. Dis-grace is a brute fact, which can only be realized. It faces itself upon us as the absurd and yet it exists as a fact and an experience. For a created being grace is grace amid the possibility of dis-grace. The human being is always a threatened being who can be dis-graced. As a history of evil, violence, destruction and cruel inhumanity, history itself is a history of dis-grace in the world; and it is fleshed out in the closing up of beings in themselves. Concrete human beings live out this drama of being simultaneously graced and dis-graced... We are both Christ and anti-Christ, openness and closedness.[18]

The challenge then is to reinterpret grace to have meaning for us today in our world where we are *dis-graced* by the way we have lived with the earth. We need to draw out the potential of this theme for the present so that we can experience the grace of God that can lead is to become more earth caring and be the source for transforming Christianity into an earth faith.

As the preceding discussion shows, it is possible to shift this ancient wisdom into the present. Boff, for example, challenges us to recognize the task of theology to "*ponder* and think about the experience of grace that is taking place today in the world and in the church".[19] He continues,

> We can try to articulate the present-day experience of grace, expressing it in a way that is appropriate for our time, accessible and acceptable to the community of faith. In this way the Christian community can identify with its past tradition while also feeling that it is creatively prolonging it. Here, the emphasis is not on talking *about* grace but on letting grace do the talking (though all talk is *about* something). In other words, we want to create an idiom and a line of reflection which will make us conscious of the divine grace in which we now live, which will allow us to detect the presence of God and his love in the world, quite apart from the fact that we may be thinking and talking about it.[20]

On the theme of grace, Elsa Tamez's description is helpful, *when we include the earth among the excluded:*

> One of Paul's intentions that generated his theological proposal of justification by faith and not by works of the law was to include the excluded in the divine project of salvation, under the same conditions that prevailed for people considered under Jewish tradition as the elect. As a theological argument supporting that intention, Paul established that all human beings are sinners, including those who have the law and those who sit in judgment over others. He proved similarly that the law does not justify or make just and therefore all people alike need the grace of God in order to do justice before humankind and before God.[21]

Grace permits us to recognize ourselves as worthy human beings who have the power to participate fully in history and of being, "capable not only of resisting but also of transforming the reality that kills, and therefore invokes only an experience of gratitude". To Tamez, life (we could add "and the earth") "is received as a gift that is worth defending", because there is totality of the human being (and again we could add "and all of creation") at stake.[22] She gives us a key to the third element in the Porto Alegre theme that refers to "transformation". Therefore God, grace and transformation are motifs that need to be woven together for an ecotheology.

Women theologians have focused on the understanding of grace in three ways. First they refer to those "moments of self-acceptance in community that provides strength for ongoing self-realization". Second, they understand grace "as conferral of dignity on persons who experience inhuman humiliation in poverty". Finally, grace is described by women theologians "as intense love for others that disposes and empowers persons to work for justice".[23] They agree that "grace occurs in connections between persons" – here they challenge traditional notions of grace coming purely and only from divine power.[24] For example Sharon D. Welch, in a very powerful book entitled *A Feminist Ethic of Risk*, speaks of the

> resilient connections with other people and the earth (that) bring joy, pain and wisdom. These resilient connections are the presence of grace. Grace can move us from resignation, bitterness and despair to passionate love and determined action... This love for others is holy and is rightly referred to as grace, a power that lifts us to a larger self and a deeper joy as it leads us to accept blame and begin the long process of reparation and recreation. Grace brings joy, not shame, the finding of self in a larger community. Grace is not the opposite of works it is the gift of being loved and loving that enables work for justice.[25]

From an eco-feminist perspective this logic needs to be broadened to the self-realization that includes all of humanity but also the earth itself, so that we have the possibility to respond to the "poverty of the earth". Grace can empower political action to ensure dignity to the earth. Grace signals the signature of the surprising and unexpected presence of God in the world – the indwelling of the divine in life and creation. God's immanence is stressed.

If grace can be perceived as that which enables us to love the earth and to work for justice, then the theme of "grace" does have the potential in the present discussion. Jay McDaniel, the Protestant theologian, has developed the concepts of "red grace" and "green grace" as possible ways in which we can develop theological resources to care for the earth.[26] I have appropriated his categories by giving them new meaning from an Indian eco-feminist theological perspective and have added "brown grace", as an additional category to respond to a new way in which eco-system peoples (Indigenous peoples and Dalits) would describe their passion to give to the land its integrity.

Green grace

An earth ethic will have to be based on *"green grace"* – the wisdom of the earth itself. McDaniel speaks of green grace as "the healing and wholeness that we find when we enjoy rich relations with plants, animals and the earth".[27] It refers specifically to the concept of the "integrity of creation". When the term was introduced for the first time in 1983 in a WCC assembly, the fate of the world was of ultimate concern. It was a time when there was a concern among the churches about the rapid deterioration of the earth and the attention to the earth was recognized as a theological imperative. As Douglas Hall, the North American ethicist, described it, "to turn towards God (theocentrism)" was simultaneously "to turn towards God's beloved world (geocentrism)."[28] Green grace, therefore, refers to "the value of all creatures for themselves, for one another and for God, and their interconnectedness in a diverse whole that has unique value for God. To forget the integrity of creation is to forget that the earth itself is a splendid whole."[29]

Larry Rasmussen posits six dimensions of the integrity of creation: the *integral functioning* and cycles from which all nature lives, ourselves included; nature's *restless self-organizing dynamism* – bio-diversity and destruction as part of the creative process; earth's treasure as *a one-time endowment* – resources are finite, limited, vulnerable, and subject to subversion and exhaustion; the *integral relation of social and environmental justice;* it names a *divine source and a certain intrinsic dignity* – that all of creation including humanity are "good" in God's eyes; and it carries the *specific ethical freight of its religious content* – the integrity of creation here means being-with as creation's own way of being.[30]

Creation's "possesses an inner cohesion and goodness" by virtue of its origin in "the will and love of the triune God".[31] This is indeed "green grace", a gift given – a thing of beauty and grace given to us to love and to cherish. This demands our active engagement to protect the earth, and this takes me to a reflection on my understanding of "red grace".

Red grace

To McDaniel "red grace" refers to the blood of Christ – a reminder that God loves us in spite of our sinfulness. He writes,

> Only when we can own our shadows can we become healers in a broken world... In the current context, our shadows include the idolatry of serving endless growth. Part of our self-awareness and our repentance must lie in finding the God of endless growth within ourselves and re-channelling his creative energies, not for exploiting others but rather for purposes of earth healing.[32]

Therefore, of prime importance is the need to situate our discourse on the earth and its distress in the frame of social, political and economic structures of injustice in our world. Challenging the neo-liberal economic project of globalization is a theological imperative, not just an ideological one. Solidarity with the poor and solidarity with the earth must be seen as two sides of the same coin that need to be addressed together and not as competing concerns. “Red grace” points us to the challenge to nurture the earth and care for the gifts of creation. It is symbolized in the blood of Christ which we celebrate through the sacraments in remembrance of the cross. This gives us the hope that God partakes of our suffering and that God does not retaliate with violence for violence or approve of the violence around us. The violence against the earth and the peoples of the earth plays out in economic violence – the violence of poverty but also of over-consumption and wealth. It challenges us to recognize that we are free to acknowledge our own greed, hatred and envy. Yet, we like other mortals are loved by God’s grace even amidst our sinfulness. The eucharistic vision accompanies us in our search for answers for the earth’s distress.

Sallie McFague reminds us that remembering the resurrection does not solve our ecological crisis; it will not tell us what to do with regard to small or large problems. But it can give us hope. Christians see the resurrection of Christ as the first day of the new creation; his resurrection is emblematic of the power of God on the side of life and its fulfilment. We are not alone as we struggle to save our planet: God is on our side.[33] But it also challenges us and our responsibility to become healers – re-channelling our creative energies not in pursuit of endless growth but for earth healing. With a new sense of adventure, we feel open to the fresh possibilities derived from God for new and hopeful futures. “Red grace” is an acknowledgment that hope for a sustainable future lies in the wisdom of the resistance struggles of communities against a development paradigm that threatens to destroy life and the earth itself.

We have examples from India of struggles for life to protect the earth. Some have been mentioned already: movements to protect the forests; and movements against mega dam projects. Additionally, there are the movements to protect bio-diversity and against nuclearization. There are also the many struggles against mining operations and there are the coastal people’s movements against over-fishing and mechanization of the fishing industry. These and many more similar movements are indeed signs of hope that God has not forsaken the earth and watches over the groaning of creation. God's grace abounds in the midst of human folly, because people *will* act for transformation, against all odds! "Red grace" is an acknowledgment of the creativity and wisdom of women – of their engagement in these efforts to affirm life. Motherhood is reclaimed. It stands for the traditions of resistance of women and their communities against a development paradigm that threatens to destroy life and the earth itself.

"Red grace" also reminds us of the creative flow of blood. In Indian culture, blood is a powerful symbol of fertility. *Kali's* rampage, in her quest to destroy evil, could be appeased only by blood sacrifices. The Khamakya temple in Guwahati, Assam is dedicated to the female genitals *(yoni)*. There is no image of the goddess in this temple but in a cave in the depths of the shrine is a *yoni*-shaped cleft in the rock, which is kept moist with a blood-like flow, caused by a natural spring. After the first monsoon rains, a great ceremony is performed when the water runs red as it mixes with the iron oxide in the rocks, symbolizing menstrual blood. The Melvaravathoor temple near Chennai is dedicated to the goddess Adiparasakthi another female fertility mother goddess. Here, women in red saris to symbolize blood, worship the gift of fertility, creativity and life.[34]

"Red grace" also reminds us that the cross is not the only symbol of atonement – Jesus throughout his life taught what it requires to live in the struggles for life of the poor and of the "new poor" – the earth. The church has tended to reduce the cross into a one-off event and it has been used to legitimize a great deal of suffering and violence in the world – particularly violence against women and children. Feminist theologians have therefore underlined their concern about the way in which the church has interpreted the cross as a symbol of vicarious sacrifice and suffering and has urged women to identify the senseless violence they experience with Christ's self-negating sacrifice.[35] As Delores Williams so powerfully expresses it, "Jesus did not come *to die* for humankind; Jesus came *to live* for humankind. Thus it is Jesus' life and his ministerial vision that redeem humans."[36] This demand to live our faith takes me to a reflection on "brown grace" which stands for ecosystem peoples and their often self-denying defence of the earth.

Brown grace

"Brown grace", a category I have added, stands for the traditions of prudent care, i.e. of the people who live in closest proximity to the earth and who give to the land its integrity. It represents the courage, the grit, the hope that sustains Narango, Sonia, Tikai, Manikura, Kosaijani... and all the other women of the Deomali Adivasi Mahila Society, whom I met in Koraput, Orissa. It represents the restlessness of those who protest against the big dams, and against the privatization of public goods, the refusal to accept genetically modified crops and other environmentally harmful ways in which "development" is being imposed on their lives. In recent years Indigenous peoples have become more articulate in expressing their deep distress at the ways in which their lives, their livelihoods and their values are being trampled on. The struggles in Bolivia against the privatization of water and the taking over of gas sources reminds us of the anxiety of Indigenous peoples all over the world, as do the actions of the market and global economic forces which erode the sustainability of the earth.

The question of the land and the protection of the integrity of the land or "brown grace" assume new meaning in the context of colonization and occupation. Musa Dube describes the imperialist interests of colonizing powers and the unfortunate nexus they had with the missionary movement when they "occupied" Africa in the 19th century. She insists that the land and its take-over are important in postcolonial readings of the Bible and other literary texts. "Here land is not just a slab of a physical body, but a web of intricately woven tales of power and disempowerment – its pages are not limited to the books, but also written on the bodies of people."[37] Dube calls for a new dialogue among women globally to move to a new international, intertextual reading so as to weave together more holistic understandings of our faith. It would pave the way for women to come together, even globally, to challenge how the Christian text has been used to legitimize occupation and colonialism.[38]

For today, such an understanding of the importance of land to the identity of peoples is of particular significance in the context of Israel's occupation of Palestine. Ateek S. Naim, the Palestinian theologian, draws our attention to how "the Bible is being quoted to give primary claim over the land to Jews. In the mind of many religious Jews and fundamentalist Christians the solution to the conflict lies in Palestinian recognition that God has given the Jews the land of Palestine forever."[39] Such a position ignores the fact that the land being occupied was not without inhabitants. Ateek links the religious life of the Palestinians with the land but stresses the importance of a reconciled community of Jews and Palestinians living on the land, together.[40]

These theologians, along with the Indigenous peoples in India, emphasize the sense of hope for a new future, where all human beings and all of creation can live in harmony and peace, together, in nurturing care of the earth. There will be a genuine sharing of space based on an ecological commitment to the sustainability of the community and the earth. We can live with grace with the earth... and the God of grace can transform the community.

From discussing this aspect of the Porto Alegre theme, I move to the second opportunity embedded in it for an earth-caring attitude. This refers to the way we image God, because I believe that the theme opens the possibility to talk of God in a new way.

The image of a God who transforms the earth with grace

Here, I reflect on metaphors for God so as to unearth the potential this offers in contributing to a theological response to the earth. In preparation for the Canberra assembly's theme, "Come, Holy Spirit – Renew the Whole Creation", the Church and Society department of the WCC organized a consultation of theologians which was held in Annecy, France, in 1988. In their report to the assembly, the drafters challenge the traditional language for God, radically. The image of God as mother, nurturing the earth was affirmed. Reference was made to the earth as the body of God:

> Instead of a king relating to his realm, we picture God as the Creator who "bodies forth" all that is, who creates not as a potter or an artist does, but more as a mother. That is to say, the universe, including our earth, and all its creatures and plants, "lives and moves and has its being" in God (Acts 17:28), though God is beyond and more than the universe. Organic images seem most appropriate for expressing both the immanence of God in and to the entire creation as well as God's transcendence of it. In the light of the incarnation the whole universe appears to us as God's body. [41]

For the WCC this was radical, because God in Christian tradition has been conceptualized as "transcendent, omnipotent and as having 'asiety' (completion) within 'himself'".[42] God has been normally cast "in male images, the symbol of divine mystery" and "is most often modelled in monarchical terms, so that God is a transcendent ruler who has dominion over the world... As a result, divine attributes were described in stark contrast to creaturely limits."[43] The Porto Alegre theme, "God, in Your Grace, Transform the World", offers us the challenge to look at our image of God in a new and earth caring way. It must be interpreted as a way in which we are set apart by God to engage with God in God's transforming acts.

Deenabandhu Manchala, a Dalit theologian, in reflecting on the theme expresses concern that this plea for God's intervention can be problematic in the context of the churches. To him, in a world where power reigns and where change of unjust structures seems impossible and where many are made to believe that there is no alternative, this mode of prayer "can only resonate with the sense of helplessness and despair". He therefore cautions,

> Resorting to prayer as the only and the final response is a common trait for Christians in many contexts, especially where they

> live as minority communities... God wants us to transform the world but we seem to resort to God to transform the world for us. *Charis*, in Greek, is a favour freely done, without claims or expectations of return. It is divine dispensation, which we only receive. This has been widely used by Christians not only to justify affluence but also inaction.[44]

Ivone Gebara takes this discussion further when she expresses concern that we have placed God outside the world and have attributed total perfection to God and imperfection to the world. She writes, "Our mindset was formed in a patriarchal tradition that posited a break or discontinuity between a Supreme Creator and all of creation."[45] In her understanding, we have set up this dualistic antithesis so as to avoid dealing with our own experiences of impurity and imperfection, our own fragility and weakness. We set up this perfect, all-powerful image of God, so as to avoid our own relative and contingent natures. In fact, we cannot imagine this perfect being far above us. "All we can do is deducing it as a hypothesis in order to continue with the life we have received."[46] She adds,

> In his name the church meted out love and punishment. In his name it intervened in people's lives. In his name it exhorted and taught the nations. In his name it admonished women and slaves to obedience. The church's voice has always been considered to represent God's person and God's power. Whereas democracies tried to speak in the name of the people, the churches claimed – and still claim – to speak in the name of God, and their actions were always thought to be for the good of the people.[47]

There is grave danger, therefore, that this assembly theme could lull us into inactivity and could kill any initiative to usher in political, social, economic and cultural transformation. Therefore, we sense the urgency to discuss the way we image God as one who encourages us to act for the sake of life. We draw inspiration from the Bible itself and discover here some metaphors for God that have been hidden behind more dominant images.

In the Bible we find multidimensional and complex metaphors for God. The New Testament presupposes the Old

Testament understanding of God, "and therein grounds its theological formulations, including its centring confession that Jesus is the Christ, the image of the invisible God (Col. 1:15). At the same time, the New Testament claims regarding Jesus Christ and the Holy Spirit result in fresh perspectives that fill out the identity of Israel's God."[48] Some of the most relevant metaphors for us here are those which image God as a compassionate, feminine, mothering God who fills the earth with grace and creative power. Such metaphors include God as shepherd (Ps. 23:1; Matt. 18:10-14); as potter (Jer. 18:1-6); as mother (Isa. 42:14, 66:13; Luke 15:8-10). The image of a child in its mother's womb or at her breast conveys a unique sense of closeness with God.[49]

Reclaiming earth-caring values in the metaphors for God

The theme of Porto Alegre offers us the possibility to reclaim some of these images of God from the Bible, which give us more earth-caring values. From an implicitly dualistic, hierarchical, individualistic and utilitarian subject-object relationship with God and the earth, we need to move intentionally to a subject-subject relationship which affirms the intrinsic value, the integrity and goodness of all of creation. The image of God as Father, or as a monarchical God, has led to the hierarchies in Christianity that had given rise not only to androcentrism and a hierarchy in creation, but also to aggressive anthropocentrism. Elizabeth Johnson writes,

> In the face of this dominant tradition, feminist theologians employ different strategies to articulate the divine. Judging Judaism and Christianity to be irredeemably male-dominated religions, some embark on an exodus from these religions to circles that connect with female deities.[50]

Third-world feminist theologians such as Yvonne Gebara, but also Kwok Pui Lan and Musa Dube have pointed out how the Western concept of the One True God as a monotheistic deity has been at the heart of imperialism and colonialism. Such an image of a warrior/colonizing God has "authorized" a destructive attitude to the conquered lands, which were occupied, industrialized and taken away from those who lived on the earth. Speaking of the Asian context and of Asian women theologian's reflections on God, Kwok Pui Lan writes,

> In a religiously pluralistic world, the ultimate, the mystery, or the sacred is known by many names. Many Asian feminist theologians believe that these different names in separate religious systems refer to realities that are totally different from that conveyed by monotheistic notions of God (Yahweh, Elohim and Allah). According to their view, while we can learn from others through religious dialogue, the Ultimate worshipped or venerated by the believers is not the same. But there is also a radical perspective arguing that the divine is a mystery, not to be pigeonholed or limited by our languages and expressions, nor boxed by our religious systems.[51]

Among Asian women the accent is on the immanence of God over against God's transcendence. Both in God's immanence and transcendence, the image is of a God found within us and in all of creation. Kwok Pui Lan underlines that in Asia it is believed that "we can come to know God through nature as well as through human history. There is no separation between 'special revelation' known through the specific Christian story and the so-called 'general revelation' known through nature and wisdom from other cultures."[52] God in India, from a liberation perspective, is in fact shaped by Indian cosmology, which affirms the interdependence of all forms of life, the dialectical harmony between humanity and the divine, between human beings and the earth and between the male and female principles.[53]

There are differences among women theologians on articulations of the divine from their different social locations. Yet on one concern there is unanimity: they all believe an earth friendly God is a God of compassion, who has "profound reverence towards life, and empathy towards those who suffer and has concern for the flourishing of all beings".[54] Here the focus is not on human beings alone but on all of life.

Another element that needs to be explored for its potential for an ecotheology is to see *the earth as the body of God.*

A.K. Ramanujan, a Tamil poet and philosopher who lived early in the last century, reflects on the earth as the body of God.[55] Sallie McFague has developed this concept further, theologically. She draws on God's reciprocal relationship with the earth and with humanity – connecting spirit and matter. God's spirit is accessible to us only in the body, i.e. the world. The world is not just nature, the good creation, but also society, the way human beings interact with one another and with nature. Exploitation and violence are thus done to the body of God, inflicted by violating the spirit when we are violent with the earth. McFague reflects on a "revived sacramentalism",

> But it is a kind of sacramentalism that is painfully conscious of the world's vulnerability, its preciousness, its uniqueness. The beauty of the world and its ability to sustain the vast multitude of species it supports is not there for the taking. The world is a body that must be carefully tended, that must be nurtured, protected, guided, loved and befriended both as valuable in itself – for like us, it is an expression of God – and as necessary to the continuation of life. We meet the world as a Thou, as the body of God, where God is present to us always and in all times and in all places. In the metaphor of the world as the body of God, the resurrection becomes a worldly, present, inclusive reality, for this body is offered to all: "This is my body."[56]

She believes that if this metaphor enters our consciousness fully, then we will begin a "different way of being in the world". We will no longer see God as disconnected from the world or the world as disconnected from God. In the context of the discussion of the WCC assembly theme, this then will inspire us to not "expect God to take care of everything, either through domination or benevolence". [57] It demands our active engagement.

Gabriele Dietrich, writing from the perspective of fisherfolk women and urban poor women in India, reflects further on the earth as the body of God. For her what is of crucial importance in an ecological theology is the "sustaining power of women who keep life going by the labour of their wombs and of their hands".[58] She reads the vision in Revelation 12 as symbolic of this interconnection between the power of women and of the earth:

> The woman clothed with the sun – the moon under her feet, and on her head a crown of twelve stars – is with child, crying out in her pangs of childbirth, in the anguish of delivery. She is persecuted by the great dragon. The child is carried to God's throne, but the woman is persecuted and flees to the desert where she is sustained. The dragon goes after her, but the earth comes to the rescue of the woman by swallowing the river poured out from the dragon's mouth. The woman in this chapter stands for the people of God, the messianic community from which the messiah is born in the birth pangs of history.[59]

Dietrich places her discussions in the context of the many forces that keep poor women and the earth in a position of enslavement and on the edge of survival. To her the dragon in the Revelation's vision represents "the destructive power, which inspires the tyrannical empires, tries to devour the child and kill the woman... It is the earth which rescues the woman from the destructive power of chaos. The earth is allied with the woman and the messianic promise."[60] She therefore believes that the labour of women will be redeemed, "by breaking down the patriarchal conditions of the production of life in the new community of the people of God, which will be rescued by the alliance with the earth."[61]

God as relatedness

From an implicitly dualistic, hierarchical, individualistic and utilitarian subject-object relationship with God and the earth we need to move intentionally to a subject-subject relationship which affirms the intrinsic value, the integrity and goodness of all of creation.[62] This will naturally draw us into understanding our image of God anew in terms of relationality. Sallie McFague offers many new images of God – images that speak of our care for each other and for all of creation. She speaks of God as Lover – of God's passionate love for the earth and for humanity; as Friend – of God's reciprocal relationship with the earth and with humanity; and as Mother – of imaging divine activities of creation and justice as feminine.[63] To this I would add God as the resisting, struggling poor woman – of God as one who brooks no injustice and who protects the earth; and finally of God as community – as the inextricable link between the divine, humanity and all of the earth. God as a mothering, nurturing woman is an important image for our times. It is necessary to see the Christian eye as a loving eye, which has a slant towards the poor – both people and the earth.[64]

Ivone Gebara too calls for a metaphor of God as *relatedness*. But then she insists that "the eco-feminist perspective opens itself to the multiplicity of forms reality takes and to reality's amazing interdependence, and in the process it reaffirms the need to avoid reducing the mysterious reality of this Sacred Body to a single image".[65] Eco-feminists would therefore contend that the many metaphors for God are the only way in which we can understand the grace of God. God intervenes here in a caring relationship not in a dominating way. However, God is not reduced to the world because God transcends human understanding therefore no one image would suffice. The model of the world as God's body encourages holistic attitudes of responsibility for the care of the vulnerable and the oppressed; it is non-hierarchical and acts through persuasion and attraction.

The theme of the Porto Alegre assembly, "God, in Your Grace, Transform the World", offers us a prayer of hope both for the earth and its children. But, as we have discovered in the last few pages, it also holds out a promise that Christianity can yet become an earth faith.

Possibilities in the way forward

The period leading up to the ninth assembly of the WCC in Porto Alegre in 2006 and the assembly itself and the programmatic directions it sets for ecumenical work in the next period are crucial for the churches so as to re-energize their commitments to the earth. We need to situate our efforts to care for the earth in the context of the work being done now of challenging the project of globalization and the trail of unsustainability it leaves behind.

Larry Rasmussen offers one way forward, which I believe is of relevance today. Drawing on the wisdom of the *oikos* (habitat earth) and the *oikoumene* or the whole-inhabited earth, he reflects on the earth as a vast but single household of life, with the capacity for survival as a sustainable habitat. Economics that is also derived from *oikos* has the basic task of ensuring *the continuation of life.* In Rasmussen's understanding, modern economics that generates the earth's present distress has moved away from the *oikos* economics. Economics now sees nature as interchangeable parts and machine-like rather than organic and communitarian. It now has the propensity to generate affluence by becoming globalized; and the firm or the corporation became the basic unit of economic agency rather than the household *(oikos).* Ecology as another derivative from *oikos* is the knowledge of life systems that is necessary for good home economics. *Oikos* members have the task of "mutual up-building of community" (St Paul) or the *oikodome* – which requires global citizenship and earth patriotism, with all the attendant duties of "choosing life" (Deut. 30:19) and living in accordance with the choice.[66]

This demands a transformation of our ways of living with each other and with the earth. This transformation has to be twofold. First comes the recognition that there is something to be learnt from the alternative cosmo-visions offered by those who live in prudent relationships with the earth. The traditions of prudence have to be listened to and recognized for their prophetic/liberative practices. These "traditional ecologists" or eco-system people, whom we have encountered in the previous pages of this book, are persons whose knowledge of local and regional life-styles can support potentially sustainable practices. The group of eco-feminist theologians who met in Geneva in 2003 urged that the next stage of the WCC's work on creation theology must be based on the documentation of "experiences of alternative communities or the traditions of prudent care of ecosystem peoples".[67]

But equally importantly, faith communities need to be ready to challenge those who call for "reform" within the present systems of global governance of environmental standards and procedures and need to instead work for restructuring of dominant economic paradigms that sustain the destruction of the earth. Faith communities have the moral responsibility of engaging in the development of alternatives to globalization and the neo-liberal economic project that under girds it.

In the World Council of Churches we have recently explored a *spirituality of resistance* as the theological basis for the search for alternatives. Here the demand is for the church and other faith communities to stand boldly in solidarity with and to work alongside those who resist developments that threaten to destroy the earth and the peoples of the earth. Konrad Raiser, former general secretary of the WCC, said this at a meeting to prepare the churches for the WCC's encounter with the international financial institutions:

> The ecumenical discussion over these past thiry years of intense involvement in the development debate and in the struggles for justice and human dignity has led us to embrace a politically engaged spirituality, which cannot simply be subsumed under the generalized notions of religious spiritual praxis which comprises everything from eastern forms of contemplation to modern programmes of spiritual self-realization. In particular, spirituality in this understanding transcends the individual and the closed horizon of the material conditions of life. It is the praxis of affirming and caring for life as a sacred gift from the Creator, which is being sustained only as it is being shared in community. By the same token, spirituality as the energy of life in all its fullness implies the commitment to resist all forces, powers and systems that reduce, deny or destroy life.[68]

The task is there before us to resist all forces, powers and systems that reduce, deny or destroy life and to "embrace a politically engaged spirituality". Each day we see the deterioration of the earth and the destruction of the community through imperialist designs and destructive political, economic and social formations. The search for a spirituality of resistance and an earth ethic can wait no longer. The concept of the earth community provides the moral framework for this to be done. But this requires a positive construction of an earth ethic *together,* provided the table is set for a dialogue of equals. It also assumes that the setting of the table in this way requires great labour and is far more difficult than current talk, of "celebrating differences" and "embracing diversity" in the interests of "community", lets on. Granting subjugated knowledge equal voice means granting subjugated people equal voice. This means power-sharing rather than "celebrating differences".[69] An ecofeminist ethic of care and of motherhood can contribute to this process – by bringing to the table the values that an eco-feminist theology is grounded in. Such an exercise demands the courage to deconstruct and reconstruct all that stands in the way of liberation and justice in our societies but also in our faith traditions, particularly in Christianity.

Now, all that is required of us is a simple and courageous communal prayer, "Yes, Creator God, in Your Grace, Transform the Earth!" If this is our prayer and this our commitment to act in transforming the earth, then listen carefully and listen well, for you will hear God's emphatic response, "If you do this, I will protect you and the earth!"

Notes

Chapter 1: Prudent Care and an Ethic of Resistance

[1] People in a mass gathering against the Subarnarekha dam project in Jharkhand (former South Bihar), *Voices of the Adivasis/Indigenous Peoples of India,* Sarini ed., Delhi, All India Coordinating Forum of the Adivasis/Indigenous Peoples, 2001, p.65.

[2] Dalits is the word used by the communities of "out-castes"/"untouchables" in India. Mohandas Gandhi gave them the name "harijans" or "children of God", but did not challenge the dehumanizing and unjust caste structure that has been religiously legitimized. The name Dalit was given to the community by their leader Dr B.R. Ambedkar and refers to their broken and downtrodden status, and has become a symbol of resistance and struggle. The system of graded subjugation called the caste system is based on rigid rules of purity and impurity, and has ensured that about 18 percent of India's population were placed outside the caste hierarchy because of their birth or occupation. Given the most menial and degrading jobs, the Dalits have continued to face injustice and violence. While the Indian constitution guarantees equality to the Dalits within the Indian society and outlaws untouchability, the practice continues. Dalit women face specific forms of violence, abuse and humiliation and have been called the "dalit of the Dalit" by Ambedkar. The caste system was regrettably carried into the church in India, and Christian Dalits continue to face injustice in the church. A vibrant and challenging Dalit national movement in society and in the church and a creative Dalit theology movement is now trying to combat this.

[3] The Indian ecologists Madhav Gadgil and Ramachandra Guha first introduced the expression "traditions of prudent *use* by eco-system people", referring to the sustainable patterns of resource use by Indigenous peoples and other who live in close proximity to the earth. So as to bring this concept in closer connection with the Christian feminist "ethic of care", I have chosen to adapt this to the expression "traditions of prudent care". See Madhav Gadgil and Ramachandra Guha, *This Fissured Land: An Ecological History of India*, Delhi, Oxford UP, 1992.

[4] David Lee, "The Natural History of the Ramayana", in *Hinduism and Ecology: The Intersection of Earth, Sky and Water*, Christopher Key Chapple and Mary Evelyn Tucker eds, Delhi, Oxford UP, 2000, p.258.

[5] Kailash C. Malhotra, "Sacred Groves", *Eco-Ethic: The INECC Newsletter,* no. 15/16, April-Sept., 2003 (Vishakapatnam, India: Indian Networks of Ethics and Climate Change), pp.18-21,24-29.

[6] O.P. Dwivedi, "Dharmic Ecology" in *Hinduism and Ecology,* 19-20.

[7] Mary McGee, quoting the ancient books of laws the *Manusmriti,* the *Yagnavalkya* and the *Vinusmriti* in "State Responsibility for Environmental Management: Perspectives from Hindu Texts on Polity", *Hinduism and Ecology,* p.93.

[8] Vandana Shiva, *Staying Alive*: *Women, Ecology and Development*, London, Zed, 1989, pp.55-56.

[9] *Ibid.*, pp.208-209.

[10] Frederique Apffel-Marglin and Pramod Parajuli, "Sacred Grove and Ecology: Ritual and Science", in *Hinduism and Ecology*, p.291.

[11] Anil Agarwal, "Can Hindu Beliefs and Values Help India Meet Its Ecological Crisis?", in *Hinduism and Ecology,* p.172.

[12] *Ibid.*, p.173.

[13] *Ibid.*, p.178.

[14] Gladys Parentelli, "Latin American Poor Women: Inherent Guardians of Life", in *Women Healing Earth: Third World Women on Ecology, Feminism, and Religion*, Rosemary Radford Ruether ed., Maryknoll NY, Orbis, 1996, p.33.

[15] Statistics gathered from various sources including government of India official sources. Quoted by Bina Agarwal in *Gender and Politics in India*, Nivedita Menon ed., Delhi, Oxford UP, 1999, pp.109-10. Also from http://web.ita.doc.gov/ete/eteinfo.nsf, accessed June 2003.

[16] Gadgil and Guha, *This Fissured Land,* p.20.

[17] Amnesty International News Service, "Work of Human Rights Defenders Threatened Because of Opposition to Industrial Projects in Orissa", AI Index: ASA 20/006/1999, 5 Feb. 1999, http://web.amnesty.org.

[18] Amnesty International News Service.

[19] Basu and Silliman citing Bina Agarwal, "Gender and Command over Property: A Critical Gap in Economic Analysis and Policy in South Asia", in *Hinduism and Ecology,* pp.431-32.

[20] *Ibid.*, p.437.

[21] Vandana Shiva, citing Ganga Ram Kalundia, leader of the *Adivasi* anti-dam movement, who was later shot and killed by the police, in *Water Wars: Privatization, Pollution and Profit*, London, Pluto, 2002, p.67.

[22] *Ibid.*, pp.105-106.

[23] *Ibid.*, pp.134-35.

[24] *Ibid.*, p.66.

[25] In a conversation with the women of the Deomali Women's Society in Semiliguda, Orissa, during a visit in Jan. 2003.

[26] Aruna Gnanadason, "Towards an Eco-feminist Theology for India", in *Women Healing Earth*, p.76.

[27] Cherabandaraju, (transl. from Telugu by C.V.Subbarao). Cited by Gadgil and Guha, *Ecology and Equity: The Use and Abuse of Nature in Contemporary India*, New Delhi, Penguin, 1995, p.vi.

[28] Gadgil and Guha, *This Fissured Land,* p.3.

[29] Larry L. Rasmussen, *Earth Community, Earth Ethics*, WCC Publications, 1996, p.181.

Chapter 2: The Struggle for Water

[1] Song by Sado Purti, activist against the Subarnarekha dam project, Jharkhand, in Purti, *Voices of the Adivasis/Indigenous Peoples of India*, Sarini ed., Delhi, All India Co-ordinating Forum of the Adivasis/Indigenous Peoples, 2001, p.25.

[2] Jawaharlal Nehru in a speech delivered in Nov. 1958 said, "I have been beginning to think that we are suffering from what we may call 'the disease of gigantism'. We want to show that we can build big dams and do big things. This is a dangerous outlook developing in India... the idea of big – having big undertakings and doing big things for the sake of showing that we can do big things – is not a good outlook at all... It is the small irrigation projects, the small industries and the small plants for electric power, which will change the face of the country far more than half a dozen big projects in half-a-dozen places" (C.V.J.Sharma ed., *Modern Temples of India: Selected Speeches of Jawaharlal Nehru at Irrigation and Power Projects*, cited by Arundathi Roy, *The Algebra of Infinite Justice*, Delhi, Viking, Penguin, 2001, p.263.

[3] *Ibid.*, pp.56-57.

[4] Shiva, *Water Wars: Privatization, Pollution and Profit,* London, Pluto, 2002, p.121.

[5] Top 10 Reasons to Oppose Water Privatization, Public Citizen, http://www.waterobservatory.org, accessed 15 June 2003.

[6] Rogate Mshana, "Water, the Source of Life: Preservation, Responsible Management and Equitable Distribution: An Ecumenical Perspective", paper presented at the European Christian Environment Network Assembly, Basel, June 2005. He quotes the www.publicintegrity.org/water/report of the International Centre for Public Integrity (ICPI).

[7] http://www.wcc-coe.org/wcc/what/jpc/earthdocs.html#water

[8] Elisabeth Moltmann-Wendel and Melanie A. May, "Feminism", in *Dictionary of the Ecumenical Movement*, Nicholas Lossky et al. eds, WCC Publications, 2002, p.471.

[9] Nivedita Menon, *Gender and Politics in India*, New Delhi, Oxford UP, 1999, p.20. This whole section is taken from Nivedita Menon's introduction to the book, and is important because she critiques the role being played by international development agencies, including Christian ones. There is a warning here that the church could replay its history of the role of control of the agenda of "development", as it had during the missionary period.

[10] Basu Amrita ed., *The Challenge of Local Feminisms: Women's Movements in Global Perspective,* Delhi, Kali for Women, 1999, p.9.

[11] Laura E. Donaldson, *Decolonizing Feminisms: Race, Gender and Empire Building*, Chapel Hill NC, Univ. of North Carolina Press, 1992, pp.3, 7.

[12] Bell Hooks, *Feminist Theory from Margin to Centre*, Boston, Southend, 1984, p.61.

[13] Mercy Amba Oduyoye, *Daughters of Anowa: African Women and Patriarchy*, Maryknoll NY, Orbis, 1995, p.3.
[14] Carolyn Merchant, *Earthcare: Women and the Environment*, New York, Routledge, 1995, p.5.
[15] Rosemary Radford Ruether ed., *Women Healing Earth: Third World Women on Ecology, Feminism, and Religion*, Maryknoll NY, Orbis, 1996, p.5.
[16] *Ibid.*, pp.3-4.
[17] *Ibid.*, p.5.
[18] *Ibid.*, p.6.
[19] *Ibid.*, p.3.
[20] Shiva, *Staying Alive,* pp.xvii-xviii.
[21] Serene Jones, *Feminist Theory and Christian Theology: Cartographies of Grace*, Minneapolis, Fortress, 2000, p.29.
[22] Shamara Shantu Riley, "Ecology is a Sistah's Issue Too: The Politics of Emergent Afrocentric Ecowomanism", in *Readings in Ecology and Feminist Theology,* Mary Heather MacKinnon and Moni McIntyre eds, Kansas City, Sheed & Ward, 1995, pp.220-21.
[23] Bina Agarwal, "The Gender and Environment Debate", in *Gender and Politics in India*, Nivedita Menon ed., Delhi, Oxford UP, 1999, p.96.
[24] *Ibid.*, p.102.
[25] *Ibid.*, p.103.
[26] *Ibid.*, p.103. See also Gabriele Dietrich's critique in "Women, Ecology and Culture", in *Gender and Politics in India.*
[27] Jones, *Cartographies of Grace*, p.30.
[28] *Ibid.*, p.40.
[29] *Ibid.*, p.46.
[30] Ivone Gebara, *Longing for Running Water: Ecofeminism and Liberation*, Minneapolis, Fortress, 1999, p.15.
[31] *Ibid.*
[32] Letty M. Russell, *Feminist Interpretation of the Bible*, Philadelphia, Westminster, 1985, p.116.
[33] *Ibid.*, p.116.
[34] *Ibid.*
[35] Sallie McFague, *Super, Natural Christians: How We Should Love Nature*, Minneapolis, Fortress, 1997, p.6.
[36] Leonardo Boff, *Ecology and Liberation: A New Paradigm*, Maryknoll NY, Orbis, 2000, p.88.
[37] Larry Rasmussen, *Earth Community, Earth Ethics,* WCC Publications, 1996, p.74.
[38] Athena Peralta, "Women and Economic Globalisation: A Discussion Paper", Justice, Peace and Creation Team, WCC, Dec. 2004, p.36.
[39] *Ibid.*, p.36.
[40] Carol Gilligan, Janie Victoria Ward and Jill McLean Taylor, "Afterword", in *Mapping the Moral Domain: A Contribution of Women's Thinking to Psychological Theory and Education,* Cambridge MA, Harvard UP, 1988. See also Carol Gilligan, *In a Different Voice: Psy-*

chological Theory and Women's Development, Cambridge MA, Harvard UP, 1982; Nel Noddings, *Caring: A Feminine Approach to Ethics and Moral Education*, Berkeley CA, Univ. of California Press, 1984; and Mary Grey, *Sacred Longings: Ecofeminist Theology and Globalization*, for her development of "the ethic of the heart" as a political project (London, SCM Press, 2003).

41 Pamela K. Brubaker, *Globalization at What Price? Economic Change and Daily Life*, Cleveland OH, Pilgrim, 2001, p.118.

42 Gebara, *Longing for Running Water*, p.21.

43 *Ibid.*, p.22.

44 *Ibid.*

45 *Ibid.*, p.23.

46 Shiva, *Staying Alive*, p.224.

47 Gabriele Dietrich, "The World as Body of God: Feminist Perspectives on Ecology and Social Justice", in *Women Healing Earth,* p.97.

48 Ann Snitow, in *Powers of Desire: The Politics of Sexuality*, New York Monthly Review, New York, NY, 1989, p.48.

49 Shamara Shantu Riley, "Ecology Is a Sistah's Issue Too: The Politics of Emergent Afrocentric Ecowomanism", in *Readings in Ecology and Feminist Theology*, p.225.

Chapter 3: Christianity as an Earth Faith

1 A protest song from Singhbhum District, Jharkhand. *Voices of the Advisai/Indigenous Peoples of India*, Sarini ed., Delhi, All India Coordinating Forum of the Adivasis/Indigenous Peoples, 2001, p.5.

2 Granvollen Final Document, *Integrity of Creation: An Ecumenical Discussion,* JPIC Resource Materials 3.2, WCC, 1988, p.9.

3 Larry Rasmussen, *Earth Community, Earth Ethics,* WCC Publications, 1996, p.xii.

4 World Council of Churches, *Now Is the Time: The Final Document and Other Texts from the World Convocation on Justice, Peace and the Integrity of Creation*, WCC, 1990, p.18.

5 See for instance Robert Booth Fowler, *The Greening of Protestant Thought*, Chapel Hill NC, Univ. of North Carolina Press, 1995. In this book Fowler argues that we need to acknowledge the diversity of Protestant eco-theologies especially when one recognizes the contrast between liberal and fundamentalist Protestants. He also defines the difference between Christian and secular environmentalists. While there is pessimism about the future in both groups, what marks Protestant environmentalism is the sense of hope and in the history, because of faith that future is in God's hands. He has a point when he asserts that there is an increase in environmental consciousness among Protestant theologians after 1970.

6 Lynn White Jr, "The Historical Roots of Our Ecological Crisis", in *Science*, 1967. Reprinted in *Readings in Ecology and Feminist Theology*, Mary Heather MacKinnon and Moni McIntyre eds, Kansas City,

Sheed & Ward, 1995, p.31. See also Carolyn Merchant, *The Death of Nature*, San Francisco, Harper & Row, 1980; Rosemary Radford Ruether, *Gaia and God: An Ecofeminist Theology of Earth Healing*, San Francisco, Harper San Francisco, 1994; Rasmussen, Earth *Community;* John E.Carroll, Paul Brockelman et al, *The Greening of Faith*, London, Univ. of New Hampshire, 1997.

[7] See Thomas Berry for his description of the different phases at which humanity has taken a "turn from the earth". *The Great Work: Our Way into the Future*, New York, Bell Tower, 1999.

[8] Mary C. Grey, *Sacred Longings: Ecofeminist Theology and Globalization*, London, SCM Press, 2003, p.12.

[9] Lance E. Nelson, "Reading the *Bhagavadgita* from an Ecological Perspective", *Hinduism and Ecology: The Intersection of Earth, Sky and Water*, Christopher Key Chapple and Mary Evelyn Tucker eds, Delhi, Oxford UP, 2000, p.129.

[10] Rasmussen, *Earth Community,* p.103.

[11] *Ibid.*, p.9.

[12] Daniel Maguire, *The Moral Core of Judaism and Christianity: Reclaiming the Revolution.* Cited by Rasmussen, Earth *Community,* p.10.

[13] Rasmussen, *Earth Community,* p.11.

[14] *Ibid.*, p.271.

[15] McFague, *Super Natural Christians: How We Should Love Nature*, Minneapolis, Fortress, 1997, p.12.

[16] Martin Robra, "Farmers Under Threat of the WTO: A Challenge to the Churches" (CCA Resource Paper http:admiralty.pacific.net.hk). Quoting Brigitte Kahl, "Fratricide and Ecocide: Re-reading Genesis 2-4". Dieter Hessel and Larry Rasmussen eds, *Earth Habitat: Eco-Justice and the Church's Response*, Minneapolis, Fortress, 2001, p.54.

[17] Rasmussen, *Earth Community*, p.228.

[18] *Ibid.*, pp.228-29.

[19] Quoted by Douglas John Hall, "Creation", *Dictionary of the Ecumenical Movement,* Nicholas Lossky et al. eds, WCC Publications, 2002, p.273. Emphasis added.

[20] *Ibid.*, p.273.

[21] Fred R. Anderson, 1986, *Presbyterian Hymnal,* hymn no. 162, Winchester Old, Este's Psalmes 1592.

[22] Carolyn Merchant, *Earthcare: Women and the Environment*, New York, Routledge, 1995, p.31.

[23] *Ibid.*

[24] Wellman, *Sustainable Communities*, WCC, 2001.

[25] Rasmussen, Earth *Community.*

[26] For this section I have drawn from the historical record of Richard D.N. Dickinson on "Development", in *Dictionary of the Ecumenical Movement*, pp.298-303.

[27] Roy H. May, "Economic Globalization", in *Dictionary of the Ecumenical Movement,* pp.488-91.

[28] Louis L.Snyder, "Josiah Strong on the Anglo Saxon Destiny, 1985", in *The Imperial Reader*, pp.122-23. Emphasis added. Cited by Musa

Dube, *Postcolonial Feminist Interpretation of the Bible*, St Louis MO, Chalice, 2000, p.5.

[29] Robert Booth Fowler, *The Greening of Protestant Thought*, Chapel Hill NC, Univ. of North Carolina Press, 1995, p.33.

[30] Jurgen Moltmann, *God in Creation: An Ecological Doctrine of Creation*, London, SCM Press, 1985, p.73.

[31] Rosemary Radford Ruether, *Gaia and God: An Ecofeminist Theology of Earth Healing*, London, SCM Press., 1992, p.21.

[32] *Ibid.*, p.21.

[33] *Ibid.*

[34] Sallie McFague, *Super Natural Christians,* p.1.

[35] Fowler, *The Greening of Protestant Thought*, p.85.

[36] *Ibid.*, p.233.

[37] *Ibid.*

[38] Geraldine S.Smyth, *A Way of Transformation: A Theological Evaluation of the Conciliar Process of Mutual Commitment to JPIC, World Council of Churches, 1983-1991*, Bern, Lang, 1995, p.146.

[39] George Mathew Nalunnakkal, *Green Liberation: Towards an Integral Ecotheology*, Delhi, ISPCK/NCCI, 1999, p.90.

[40] *Ibid.*, p.141.

[41] Ivone Gebara, *Longing for Running Water: Ecofeminism and Liberation*, Minneapolis, Fortress, 1999, p.46.

[42] Hyun Kyung oral sharing during a small discussion group of eco-feminists theologians on "Women and Creation" held at the John Knox Centre, Geneva, by the Justice, Peace and Creation team of the WCC, 4-8 July 2003.

[43] Rasmussen, *Earth Community,* p.235.

[44] *Ibid.*, p.236.

[45] Tink Tinker, in an oral dialogue on the theology of life at the German Protestant Kirchentag (Church Day) Leipzig, in 1997.

[46] Rasmussen, *Earth Community*, p.239.

[47] *Ibid.*, p.107.

[48] *Ibid.*, p.238.

[49] Tamara Grdzelidze, "How Does the Orthodox Church Respond to Ecological Problems?", in *The Ecumenical Review*, vol. 54, no. 3, July 2002.

[50] Rasmussen, *Earth Community*, pp.238-39.

[51] From the conclusions and recommendations given by the inter-Orthodox conference on environmental protection held in Crete in Nov. 1991. Quoted by Grdzelidze, "How Does the Orthodox Church Respond to Ecological Problems", p.213

[52] Genadios Limouris, quoted by Geraldine S. Smyth, O.P., *A Way of Transformation: A Theological Evaluation of the Conciliar Process of Mutual Commitment to JPIC, World Council of Churches, 1983-1991*, Bern, Peter Lang, 1995, p.67.

[53] Smyth, *A Way of Transformation*, p.66.

[54] *Ibid.*, p.66.

[55] Gebara, *Longing for Running Water*, p.157.

[56] *Ibid.*, p.167.
[57] Hall, "Creation", p.271.
[58] *Ibid.*
[59] *Integrity of Creation – An Ecumenical Discussion*, p.3.
[60] *Ibid.*, p.16.
[61] *Ibid.*
[62] Hall, "Creation", p.274.
[63] Smyth, *A Way of Transformation,* p.69.
[64] *Ibid.*
[65] Rasmussen, *Earth Community*, p.98.
[66] David G. Hallman, *Spiritual Values for Earth Community*, WCC Publications, 2000, p.13.
[67] David J. Wellman, *Sustainable Communities*, 2001, pp.1-7. There are several WCC documents that Wellman refers to that would trace WCC's discussions on the terms. I have not gone into detail in this discussion as it is beyond the scope of this book.
[68] The term sustainable development gained prominence in a report entitled *Our Common Future*, produced by Gro. Bruntland Harlem, then prime minister of Norway, in her capacity as chair of the UN World Commission on Environment and Development. She defined sustainable development as "the management of human use of the biosphere so that it may yield the greatest sustainable benefit to present generations while maintaining the potential to meet the needs and aspirations of future generations". The report also claims that "the environment does not exist as a special sphere separate from the actions, ambitions and needs of man (sic!). Attempts to defend the environment without taking into consideration the unrest and worries of man have given the word environment a ring of naivety in certain political circles. The word development has also been reduced by many to refer to very limited areas, namely what poor countries should do to become wealthier, and has thus been dismissed by many as being of interest to specialists only. But the environment is what we will live on and development is what we do to try to improve our situation within this our common home. The two cannot be separated."
[69] Quoted by Wellman, *Sustainable Communities,* p.185.
[70] Rasmussen, *Earth Community*, pp.15-16.
[71] *Ibid.*, p.1.
[72] "Corporate Accountability – A Matter of Sustainable Justice", a Fact Sheet for the WSSD – from the Ecumenical Team, http://www.wcc-coe.org/wcc/what/jpc/corp-account. Internet. Accessed Sept. 2003.
[73] Fact Sheet for the WSSD.
[74] Klaus Schwab, "Get Back to Business", in *Newsweek,* 5 May 2003, New York.
[75] Martin Robra, "People's Struggles for Life Are a Source of Inspiration for an Enriching Spirituality", *National Council of Churches Review,* vol. 122, no. 1, Jan-Feb. 2002, Nagpur, India: NCCI Publication, pp.3-8.
[76] A summary of the international conference, Faith and Ecology 2001: Land, Water, Air, NCCI Review, pp.109-20.

[77] Quoted by Athena Peralta, p.41.

[78] *Now Is the Time: The Final Document on Justice, Peace and the Integrity of Creation,* Seoul, Republic of Korea, 5-12 March 1990, WCC, 1990.

[79] "The Jo'burg-Memo: Fairness in a Fragile World", *Memorandum for the World Summit on Sustainable Development*, Wolfgang Sachs et al. eds, Heinrich Boll Foundation www.joburgmemo.org) April 2002. Internet. Accessed July 2003.

[80] "The Jo'burg-Memo".

[81] The World Social Forum has become a yearly event when social movements gather to assert that another world is possible. It began as an alternative to the World Economic Forum, which was set up by those with a stake in global capitalism to ensure that economic growth and trade are able to flourish. The WSF, which has traditionally met in Porto Alegre, Brazil, now asserts alternatives to globalization and does not perceive itself simply as an anti-globalization project.

[82] Martin Robra, "Trust in the Social Logic of the Gospel", in *The Ecumenical Review,* vol.56, no. 1, Jan. 2004, pp.16-17.

[83] Rasmussen, Earth *Community,* p.351.

[84] Introduction to the *Dossier on Working on Theology of Life*, WCC Unit III, Justice, Peace and Creation, 1998, pp.8-9.

[85] "Resisting Domination – Affirming Life: The Challenge of Globalization", Policy Reference Committee II report, appendix II: Globalization, *Together on the Way: Official Report of the Eighth Assembly of the World Council of Churches,* Diane Kessler ed., WCC Publications, 1999, p.259.

[86] *Ibid*., p.259.

[87] *Ibid*., p.260.

[88] James Nash, *Loving Nature: Ecological Integrity and Christian Responsibility*, cited by Rasmussen, *Earth Community*, pp.108-109.

[89] *Ibid*., p.79.

[90] Michel Gelobter, "Urban Environmental Justice", cited by Rasmussen, *Earth Community*, p.79.

[91] Study guide on *Transformative Justice: Being Church and Overcoming Racism. A Resource Guide*, Justice, Peace and Creation team, WCC, 2003.

[92] Rosemary Radford Ruether, "Ecofeminism: Symbolic and Social Connections of the Oppression of Women and the Domination of Nature", in *Ecofeminism and the Sacred*, Carol J.Adams ed., New York, Continuum, 1995, p.21.

[93] A small meeting was held at the John Knox Centre, Geneva, 4-8 July 2003, on women and creation, which served both to develop the WCC's work on creation theology and was also as part of my dissertation project. The group of ten women theologians were mostly ecofeminist theologians: Puleng Lenka Bula (South Africa); Dorothy Munyakho (Kenya); Kwok Pui Lan (Hong Kong); Hyun Kyung (South Korea) ; Prasanna Kumari (India) ; Sirirat Pusurinkham (Thailand) ;

Rosemary Radford Ruether (USA) ; Heather Eaton (Canada) ; Ivone Gebara (Brazil) ; and Judy Ress (Chile/USA). Martin Robra and Aruna Gnanadason (WCC staff)

94 Rosemary Radford Ruether, "Ecofeminism and the World Council of Churches", manuscript.

Chapter 4: Towards an Eco-feminist Theology

1 Sado Purti, Indigenous activist during the campaign against the Subarnarekha dam projects in Jharkhand (former South Bihar) in 1991-1992. Maghe Parab and Ba-Parab are two places submerged by the dam. Sado Purti, *Voices of the Adivasis/Indigenous Peoples of India*, Delhi, All India Co-ordinating Forum of the Adivasis/Indigenous Peoples, 2001,p.14

2 Jay McDaniel, "The Sacred Whole: An Ecumenical Protestant Approach", *The Greening of Faith: God, the Environment and the Good Life*, John E.Carroll, Paul Brockelman and Mary Westfall eds, London, Univ. Press of New England, 1997, p.107.

3 George E. Tinker, "An American Theological Response to Ecojustice", in *Defending Mother Earth: Native American Perspectives on Environmental Justice*, Jace Weaver ed., Maryknoll NY, Orbis, 1996, p.156.

4 Rosetta E. Ross, "Grace", in *Dictionary of Feminist Theologies,* Letty Russell and J. Shannon Clarkson eds, Louisville KY, Westminster John Knox, 1996, p.133.

5 Johannes Brosseder, "Grace", in *Dictionary of the Ecumenical Movement*, Nicholas Lossky et al. eds, WCC Publications, 2000, p.497.

6 Ross, "Grace", p.133.

7 Brosseder, "Grace", p.497.

8 David A. DeSilva, "Grace",in *Dictionary of the Bible,* David Noel Freedman ed., Grand Rapids MI, Eerdmans, 2000, p.525.

9 José Míguez Bonino cited by Elsa Tamez, *The Amnesty of Grace: Justification by Faith from the Latin American Perspective*,.transl. Sharon Ringe, Nashville TN, Abdingdon, 1993, pp.32-33.

10 Brosseder, "Grace", p.498.

11 *Ibid*., pp.499-500.

12 Tamez, *The Amnesty of Grace,* 132-133.

13 Leonardo Boff, *Liberating Grace*, Maryknoll NY, Orbis, 1979, p.6.

14 *Ibid*., 5-6.

15 See particularly, Leonardo Boff, *Ecology and Liberation: A New Paradigm*, Maryknoll NY, Orbis, 2000; and Ivone Gebara, *Longing for Running Water: Ecofeminism and Liberation*, Minneapolis, Fortress, 1999.

16 Larry Rasmussen, *Earth Community, Earth Ethics*, WCC Publications, 1996, p.143.

17 Leonardo Boff, *Liberating Grace*, Maryknoll NY, Orbis, 1979, p.5.

18 *Ibid*., p.4.

19 *Ibid*., p.5.

[20] *Ibid.*

[21] Elsa Tamez, The *Amnesty of Grace,* p.124.

[22] *Ibid.*, p.134.

[23] Ross, "Grace", p.133.

[24] *Ibid.*, p.134.

[25] Sharon D. Welch, *A Feminist Ethic of Risk*, rev. ed., Minneapolis, Fortress, 2000, pp.173-74.

[26] McDaniel, "The Sacred Whole", pp.114-15.

[27] *Ibid.*, p.115.

[28] Douglas John Hall, cited by Rasmussen, *Earth Community,* p.98.

[29] Jay McDaniel, cited by Rasmussen, *Earth Community,* p.99.

[30] *Ibid.*, pp.99-107.

[31] *Integrity of Creation – An Ecumenical Discussion,* Granvollen, Norway, 25 Feb.-3 March 1988, WCC-Church and Society, 1989, p.3.

[32] McDaniel, "The Sacred Whole", p.114.

[33] Sallie McFague, *Life Abundant: Rethinking Theology and Economy for a Planet in Peril*, Minneapolis, Fortress, 2000, p.170.

[34] Aruna Gnanadason, "Reclaiming Motherhood: In Search of an Ecofeminist Vision", in *Sustainability and Globalization*, Julio de Santa Ana ed., WCC Publications, 1998, p.139.

[35] See Aruna Gnanadason, *No Longer a Secret: The Church and Violence against Women*, WCC Publications, 2nd ed. 1997. The World Council of Churches has for the past two decades been working on the issue of violence against women and the theological justifications that are often given by the church to condone the violence women experience. The cross has been particularly problematic because it has been used to legitimize the sacrifice of women both in domestic and church circles. A special campaign entitled "On the Wings of a Dove", scheduled to coincide with the secular yearly campaign "16 Days of Activism against Violence against Women" 25 November-10 December 2004, focused the churches' attention on overcoming violence against women and children. Many women have written on this deep concern, particularly important are the theological contributions of Delores S. Williams, *Sisters in the Wilderness: The Challenge of Womanist God-Talk*, Maryknoll NY, Orbis, 1993.

[36] Delores Williams, "Atonement", in *Dictionary of Feminist Theologies*, p.18.

[37] Musa Dube, *Postcolonial Feminist Interpretation of the Bible*, St Louis MO, Chalice, 2000, p.119.

[38] Several new post-colonial literary scholars including Kwok Pui Lan and Mrinalini Sebastian from Asia, complement Dube's work on a post-colonial interpretation of the Bible.

[39] Naim S. Ateek, "A Palestinian Perspective: Biblical Perspectives on the Land", in *Voices from the Margin: Interpreting the Bible in the Third World*, R.S. Sugirtharajah ed., Maryknoll NY, Orbis, 1995, p.268.

[40] *Ibid.*, p.276.

41 Charles Birch, William Eakin, Jay B. McDaniel eds, *Liberating Life: Contemporary Approaches to Ecological Theology*, Maryknoll, Orbis, 1990, p.279.

42 Daphne Hampson, "Monotheism", in *Dictionary of Feminist Theologies,* p.186.

43 Elizabeth A. Johnson, "God", in *Dictionary of Feminist Theologies,* p.128.

44 Deenabandhu Manchala, presentation on the Porto Alegre theme, WCC staff week of meetings, Nov. 2003, unpublished manuscript.

45 Ivone Gebara, *Longing for Running Water: Ecofeminism and Liberation*, Minneapolis, Fortress, 1999, p.110.

46 *Ibid.,* p.111.

47 *Ibid.,* p.113.

48 Terence E. Fretheim, "God", in *Dictionary of the Bible*, p.511.

49 *Ibid.*

50 Johnson, "God", p.129.

51 Kwok Pui Lan, *Introducing Asian Feminist Theology*, Cleveland, Pilgrim, 2000, pp.67-68.

52 *Ibid*., pp.75-76.

53 Aruna Gnanadason, "Toward a Feminist Eco-theology for India", in *Women Healing Earth: Third World Women on Ecology, Feminism, and Religion*, Rosemary Radford Ruether ed., Maryknoll NY, Orbis, 1996, pp.74-81.

54 Pui Lan, *Introducing Asian Feminist Theology,* p.77.

55 Vinay Dharwadker ed., *The Collected Essays of A.K.Ramanujan*, New Delhi, Oxford UP, 1999.

56 Sallie McFague, Models *of God: Theology for an Ecological, Nuclear Age*, London, SCM Press, 1987, p.77.

57 *Ibid.*

58 Gabrielle Dietrich, "The World as the Body of God: Feminist Perspectives on Ecology and Social Justice", in *Women Healing Earth,* pp.92-93.

59 *Ibid*., p.93.

60 *Ibid.*

61 *Ibid.*

62 McFague, *Super Natural Christians: How We Should Love Nature,* Minneapolis, Fortress, 1997, pp.7-9.

63 McFague, *Models of God.*

64 McFague, *Super Natural Christians,* p.169.

65 Gebara, *Longing for Running Water*, p.127.

66 Rasmussen, *Earth Community,* pp.93-95.

67 Report of the meeting on women and creation, 4-8 July 2003, Geneva, John Knox Centre, manuscript.

68 Konrad Raiser, "Spirituality of Resistance", paper presented at the WCC internal encounter of churches, agencies and other partners on the World Bank and IMF, Geneva, 12 Sept. 2003.

69 Larry Rasmussen, "Song of Songs: Ecumenical Christianities as Earth Faiths", power-point presentation, June 1999.